The Poetry Review

The Poetry Society, 22 Betterton Street, London WC2H 9BX

The Poetry Review

The Poetry Society, 22 Betterton Street, London WC2H 9BX
Tel: +44 (0)20 7420 9883 • Fax: +44 (0)20 7240 4818
Email: poetryreview@poetrysociety.org.uk
www.poetrysociety.org.uk

Editor: Maurice Riordan
Production: Michael Sims

ISBN: 978-1-900771-93-1 ISSN: 0032 2156
Cover illustration Stuart Daly, www.stuartdaly.com

. . .

SUBMISSIONS
For details of our submission guidelines,
please visit the *The Poetry Review* section of
www.poetrysociety.org.uk

ADVERTISING
To advertise, visit www.poetrysociety.org.uk
or contact Oliver Fox on
+44 (0)20 7420 9886,
email: marketing@poetrysociety.org.uk

BOOKSHOP DISTRIBUTION
Central Books, 99 Wallis Road, London
E9 5LN, UK. Tel: 0845 458 9925
or visit www.centralbooks.com

PBS EXCLUSIVE BOOK SUPPLY SERVICE
Readers of *The Poetry Review* can receive many
of the books featured in the magazine post-free
by mail order from the Poetry Book Society.
To order, tel: +44 (0)20 7831 7468,
Mon-Fri, quoting *The Poetry Review*.

SUBSCRIPTIONS & SALES
UK individuals: £34 / Europe: £44
Rest of the World: £49
(all overseas delivery is by airmail)
Single issue: £8.95 plus postage.
Order from www.poetryreview.org.uk or contact
Paul McGrane on +44 (0)20 7420 9881.
Pay by cheque (sterling and US dollar
cheques only), credit card or Direct Debit.

The Poetry Review is also available on audio CD.

The Poetry Review is the magazine of
The Poetry Society and was first published in 1912.
A subscription to *The Poetry Review* is included as
part of membership of The Poetry Society. It is also
on sale in leading bookshops. A digital version of
the magazine is also available. Views expressed in
The Poetry Review are not necessarily those of The
Poetry Society; those of individual contributors
are not necessarily those of the Editor.
Charity Commission No. 303334.

CONTENTS

Poems

Poems from Poetry

Prose

Poems

Reviews

EDITORIAL

"Life ain't fair," remarked the lioness – her jaws opening for the purpose – to the doomed wildebeest. It's no different in the furiously Darwinian world of poetry. Herds of poets nightly roam the plains of Twitter and Facebook, where there is scant cover. Reputations are savaged and egos mutilated during the sleepless hours. Only those most nimble, cunning – and lucky – escape the bloody slaughter.

I exaggerate. Even so, the poetry world is a competitive place. Many thousands of mainly serious, intelligent, properly ambitious people vie to have their poems read, heard, liked, remunerated. The internet has opened up more possibilities to get one's work aired. But enthusiasms flare and fade quickly online. The printed page, though it's no guarantee against oblivion, remains coveted space.

For a publication such as this, it's important to try to be fair. We inherit inequities not only of race and gender, but also of education, geography, age, looks, so many indeed that an effective logarithm of fairness seems impossible. And every individual who takes to writing poetry is, in any case, a minority of one. It's important to be receptive to those who are starting out, or have lacked success as yet. And it's equally important to notice older poets who may have fallen from fashion. A current phenomenon indeed is the late blossoming of poets. In this issue you will find examples of what John Berryman referred to (in tribute to William Carlos Williams) as "mysterious late excellence".

An easy way for an editor to be representative is to request poems from a spectrum of poets. Such 'soliciting' of contributions is fine at creating a semblance of diversity, of the kind readily recognised by funding bodies. But it has its drawbacks. One is that poets are canny beasts and send inferior work to those importunate editors, while they reserve the good stuff for more aloof outlets. It also negates the taste of the editor, which can be one true thing in a partisan world. It prevents that primary experience that lies at the heart of all imaginative culture, the free surrender of one susceptible mind to another. And it would remove, incidentally, the main reward of editing for me: the pleasure of finding a new poem from someone I've never heard of.

So, it's a shame to pre-empt, or bias, the exercise of editorial judgement. But it is still possible for a magazine to work at building an open arena. In the prose pages, one has control over the range of poetry reviewed or commented on. It should be a space where perhaps neglected books are valued – and where celebrated or hyped books are, on occasion, put under scrutiny. This establishes a forum of lively and honest argument, and that encourages, in turn, the feeling among poets seeking recognition that at least they will get a fair hearing.

In intent, this is the editorial spirit we adhere to. In keeping with this spirit, *TPR* is embarking on a series of joint editorships, which *per se* involve a degree of diversity. Emily Berry will join me in editing the Summer issue. Berry has received wide acclaim for her debut collection, *Dear Boy*. She is also a seasoned editor already. We're hopeful the partnership will extend the appeal of the magazine and enhance its quality.

Maurice Riordan

DAVID HART

No faun

Then in the afternoon no faun,
no faun had been promised, a whimsy only,
sight of a faun would please the soul.

Not enough leap for a distant sighting –
good conscience anyway would not allow it,
did we *hear* a faun that day? No, we did not.

Without fulfilment of faun whimsy,
without on that wayward afternoon a faun,
quick now, hide and be sad alone.

The long wait and the snarl of a quick sunset,
no faun had leapt, night –

Now that the hut

Now that the hut is falling away into the valley,
leaving flying splinters, leaving books flapping,
I feel very silly, I want to make a decent claim
        on my own integrity,
at the very least ask why and receive a tolerable
        reply innerly.

My mouth is dry-minded. There was more than
        one room,
or say one room and a large annexe, name it annexe,
and there was a wash shack nearby, also now
        slipping away.

Now I know what a wheeze life is, I watch, my back
against a flat white rock, home flown, gone through
        smudged air.
The whirlwind came, opened the door without
        waiting and calling out
          Hello, hello!

Pages flapping

I leave my few books outside flipping and flapping,
wandering past I glance at a page of a book as the breeze
    opens it to me.
After a waltzing walk I glance at the flapping page
  of another. Each time
 I am influenced. For what? Enchantment.

To speak true, I walk up and down hoping to see angels
descending and ascending, one playing a tabor, another
a drone pipe, a third a slide trumpet or a golden shawm.
Not for me to say, only to accept as they move about the
air of my garden an angel with a fiddle, another with
a tromba marina, there may be a transverse flute or a
duo of clapper bells and surely a whole choir singing.

To speak as conscience dictates, there is a friendly squirrel
   comes often to the hazel
 in the corner of my patch, stays for a moment
   while I tell it my news, as when
I had been down the lane to pick blackberries and
   there was that time when I had fallen
    into a muddly puddle.

At the break

At the break for tea and ginger biscuits he
collapsed stuttering *Amen shit ok shit so*, avowed thus
by those who had stood with him, they had
walked about then rehearsing to memorise
Amen shit ok shit so, deepening it.

The next day
some demurred, to *Amen shit shit ok so*, or *Ok shit
Amen so* and other versions, one professor
wrote and passed around *Amen shit shit ok so* and
established it on the internet. Theory

has taken hold, one journal so far has
devoted a whole issue, and an old scholar can
still be seen walking the park crying into
      a starched white hankie.

Taking note

I take note in myself
of my weighty coat,
I am in exile in it,
I wander and the coat

comes along with me.
Sometimes it seems
the coat decides
and I find myself

in exile differently.
Today I have found
in one of its deep
and dark pockets

rotting blackberries.
I know an old man
who wakes and sleeps
on the railway station.

He told me a dream:
he was lying on a cloud
close to death, he
bathed in the scent

of honeysuckle, and now
is dead. I wander now
ever more alone, cold,
in my weighty coat.

A.K. BLAKEMORE

introversion.forum

as if cut from the throat, in the cyan clarity
of the moments that follow intercourse we feel most keenly aware of the
    ice-cream men and
kites snapping taut against the wind. how far below? how many storeys up
    are we? i kiss your eyelids. i saw it in a movie.

ah, bonsai.

like a calm torturer, laying out my bijou implements
every day.

i think my lover
should be a little tree.

lovers

i was frustrated by
the way he received fellatio,

very blonde underarm –

with the passivity
of a teddy bear of a dog –

how!
(tight-clasping memory!)

no one was allowed to hurt him
but me.

our town

the dead rat was uninjured.
rigor mortis had set in, freezing the tail to a loop about
the circumference of my forearm.
probably

it had eaten poison. when it rains (which it sometimes does
for days) the snails
come out, in liquid
eye-tiaras and

at night i saw a car with blue
under-lights parked
outside the restaurant. another place sells fruit loaves and
secondhand bridesmaids' dresses.

i don't know where to buy khat yet. salvia
i do. ask me about my tattoos.
red-and-white striped

tube top. heart-shaped padlock.
i didn't notice him putting his hand
there. it was raining.

but hold me
like something that shakes
when it goes unheld. you've trained
your body not to take up the space
it ought to take –

and everyone else we've ever met
would die if they came to this place.

RACHEL PIERCEY

An Overblown Poem About Love

Because it can see for two miles
I have set a peacock on the roof.

Its body is like a distilled sea
but more tempestuous and noisy.

Certain folk it regards as friends,
and then it hurries down to strut

around the dusty moat of yard
and make a revelation of its tail,

or simply does not pause in prising
insects from the slatted wood.

In many ways it is well trained.
I mean, it is trained in many ways

by a variety of guests,
so it is tactically efficient.

Take this shape on the horizon:
slow, resolving, barrelling

into sight, towards the fence,
and how the peacock tenses, trembles,

starts to strike out with its claws,
and how it crashes through the yard

to scream at the stranger, gaining fast.
I'm contemplating something bad.

I have one hand upon the latch.
I have one hand upon the axe.

Post-film,

he has the pleasant sense of being watched.
The cameras are trained on his back
as he walks naturally towards the gents,
opening the door in a manner
which implies upper-body strength.
The way to describe what he is doing
is *pissing*, or maybe *taking a slash*.
Even the way he washes his hands is interesting,
half slapdash, peering casually in the mirror,
half attending to the build-up of germs.
It suggests just the occasional rearing of nerves.
From this angle, all the girls in his past
are beautiful, sunlit and melancholic
and all the girls in his future are beautiful
and sunlit too. And every mistake
is softened and understandable. And even the rain
on his face will be the applauding of hands.

Heraclitus Heart

I asked the lonely stretch of river
to tell me more about my lover;
he loved this place when he was younger.
The river hunched its chilly shoulder:
Remember the one about the river?
The water here is not his water.
The water's always flowing further
and can't be said to be the river.
I tried again and asked the water
about the banks my love leaned over
which made the rearing waves declare:
Do not define me by my borders!
A lake might give such easy answers
but only the sea has the mouth of the river.
I bent towards the deepest boulders
and asked if they could make him clearer
but the bed blew clouds into the water:
The things that build up under here
are solely for the river's ears.
So I asked my lover about the river
he pitched and skimmed and floated over
but looking round I found him nowhere:
remember the one about the lover.

LEONTIA FLYNN

Catullus 6

F-, speaking as a friend here, your new hottie
must be *incredibly* rough around the edges
or you couldn't contain yourself – you'd spill the beans!
I have to deduce, then, that some anorexic
scrubber you're none too proud of's got your fancy.
Look, none of this lying about *lonely nights*
cold as a widow, when your bed itself –
reeking of perfume, draped with God-knows-what,
the pillows on *both sides* – clincher – battered flat,
might, from the groaning racket that it's making,
creak through the door right now to prove you wrong!
There isn't any point you keeping quiet:
why? Would you look so comically fucked-out
if not engaged in some new bit of boldness?
Whoever you've got hidden, nice or naughty,
tell me! I want the pair of you, laid bare,
yes, cried from the rooftops of my poetry!

Catullus 8

Give it up moron: forget it all, let it go.
Chalk up among your losses what's lost now for good.
Once, every day's fierce sun blazed madly for you
when, hot on her heels, you'd scuttle off after *her*
– the girl that you loved, like *nobody* has been loved;
to where, back then – oh yes – it was all fun and games
to do what you wanted, which she didn't *not* want
much... so each day's sun blazed in a shiny blue sky.
Now she's said 'no' for real, accept it; don't fight it.
Don't chase after shadows. Don't dwell on your crappy life
but make up your mind to endure this – ride it out!
Do you see – Goodbye! Goodbye! – how I'm riding this out,
sweetheart? This stiff upper lip? And you'll be sorry
when I don't come scampering after you again,
and nobody does, and no one calls you gorgeous...
You heartless cow. Let me wish you appalling luck
in future affairs: who'll love you? Who'll you love back?
And who will get to kiss you – God! – whose lips you'll bite...
while, make no mistake, I'll *do this!* I'll ride it out...

Catullus 46

Now Spring has fetched the chill out of the days
once more – and now the savage equinox
rolls over at the whisper of a breeze –
for the love of God let's get out of these camps
and landlocked fields: forsaken, fecund, sweaty
to clarify our lives in the bright city.
Comrades, I've itchy feet. I've itchy socks.
My mind is wandering off the beaten track.
And so goodbye, goodbye my gang of 'chums'
though long ago, as one, we left our homes
now diverse, solitary ways will take us back.

Catullus 27

Service: you there, boy pouring pinot grigio
get me a glass of something... more full bodied.
Our Lady of Misrule says that's an order
(and she can talk, being already blootered).
And as for you ice- and water-bearers, go
find duller people's drinks to ruin: faders,
lightweights and killjoys: make mine undiluted.

MILES BURROWS

The Butcher's Wink

K.J. Elderman, FAMILY BUTCHER,
had an establishment at the corner of Holbrook Road
that gave this part of Pinner the look of a *quartier*
with its awning, its blackboards of chalked offers
and the blue aprons, white pork pie hats.
There was an atmosphere of joviality
among gossiping housewives, excited
by so much raw meat cut from different angles.
Bethany and I were 'seeing' each other
or at least I was looking at her a lot
through a haze of cigarette smoke and Tibetan Buddhism
and popped in here for a pound of ham for lunch
while Bethany hovered in the doorway in her jeans.
Elderman sliced the ham, nibbling small bits
in his usual way, and handed it to me wrapped
in greaseproof, with a twinkle and a wink.
As if he saw this episode in my life
sketched not by Graham Greene as I'd supposed
but Alan Ayckbourn. Who knows what a butcher sees
from his window? I never went back.
Till decades later I wander in here again.
And he slices the ham, nibbling a few bits,
and hands it to me without letting go for a second,
as if he's shy of putting the question into words.

But those unheard

The next poem we can't actually see.
In fact it may not be there at all.
But if it was there it would solve several problems
in the poems that we can see. We infer its existence
from what we believe to be its effects.
It may be a completely new kind of poem
or something similar, that has leverage
on existing poems, being itself unreadable
and extremely heavy and moving at a high speed.
Heavy invisible rapid poem-like entities,
which may never be seen or felt, almost certainly underlie
existing poems, and may outweigh them
as the dead outnumber the living.
And they have an activity, as the dead
can bend existing poems and hold them together.
But these are not dead poems
(we haven't got a name for them yet).
They may explain shivering, wrinkles, or otherwise unexplained anomalies
in poems we thought we understood. Lacunas,
leanings, hesitations, small lapses in grammar, odd coinings,
unexplained dashes or ashes where commas might be expected,
a wandering semicolon. Misspellings we pretended to ignore.
Two instances of hapax legomena in seventeenth-century Siamese poems
could be explained by a heavy unwritten poem-like entity (about the size
    of Denmark)
passing rapidly very close to them or through them.
In fact the whole field of textual criticism
has become much more exciting
as we study here underground in darkness and close to absolute silence
poems we thought we remembered.

In Bloomsbury Square

I could write a biography.
Of myself.
Or even of some different person.
But who else might be of interest?
Nelson has been done so many times.
They could make a pillar for me
and I would scorn the pillar
and be simply lying down on my back relaxing
at the base of the pillar
eating some olives from a backpack
and wondering what the time was.
And people would look and say
"Are you one of those people who dress up as a statue?
You're like the dead girl in the wrenched-open coffin
with her grey dead baby, when Julie Christie
asks Terence Stamp 'Do you love me?'
And he says 'She is more to me
Than you are, or were, or ever could be.'
How old are you? What's it like being a dead poet?"
It's very like being a live one.
It's trying to play the piano
with breakfast honey still stuck between your fingers.

HOWARD ALTMANN

Notes in the Dark

I must forgive time its infinite perfection and consummate deceit.
I must forgive humanity its unwieldy mass and malleable intent.
I must forgive history its selective disclosure and indiscriminate litany.

Whether nature listens more than it speaks, touches more than it is
    touched on this the rains can fill my ears.
Whether trading an apple for a pear, a bird for a cloud, a truth for a
    revelation was good business I shall not belabor.
Whether ambition plumbed the depths, hollowed the mystery, or potted
    the silence I am resting on a ledge.

If my identity swims in old man's clothes or wades in child's feet, silly it
    seems to water that now.
If much more remains to discover about family and friends, may the
    query's seed scatter me bare.
If neither wind nor snow will sweep the voices, have the undulating sea
    pick up the monologue.

That fear holds binoculars and loneliness the focus, the shrouded moon
    knows well how to adjust the clouds.
That days can be gray and people grayer, the demonstration in the black
    sky can go on diminishing the white in my eye.
That rise of self is landscape and horizon, I must forgive myself for falling
    and falling in the light.

NICK LAIRD

Team Me

I get very bored of having to respond
to the circumstances of my life.
I'm fed up following my ego round.

I remember the feeling from being a lawyer,
sat there opposite some client thinking
I just can't represent this cunt much longer.

Most nights we meet each other face to face –
at civil dusk, in defeat, my little regent
standing in Gristedes' dairy aisle or the lower

field where the red clay banks and falls away,
and the stream that feeds the Ballinderry slows
on shallow gravels. Wherever. On his own.

Always with the narrow back aimed like a shield
against me, his shadow like a bracket or a lever
twice as long as him and half as thin

keeping us forever locked perpendicular to earth.
He turns. Bat fangs. Bowl cut. Such pretty little
ears that hold the crown, a ripped green cracker hat

from Christmas 1983. O my petty liege.
My bliss and darling enmity. My dearest nemesis.
When he spots us now and slopes across,

affecting a limp, because he's depressed,
what I say when he asks how it went on the whole
is *no really no really no you were amazing.*

Poems from *Poetry*

RAE ARMANTROUT

Asymmetries

I'm thinking about you and you're humming while cutting a piece of wood.
I'm positive you aren't thinking about me which is fine as long as you
aren't thinking about yourself. I know and love the way you inhabit
this house and the occasions we mutually create. But I don't know
the man you picture when you see yourself walking around
the world inside your head and I'm jealous
of the attention you pay that person
whom I suspect
of being devious.

CHEN CHEN

I'm not a religious person but

God sent an angel. One of his least qualified, though. Fluent only in
Lemme get back to you. The angel sounded like me, early twenties,
unpaid interning. Proficient in fetching coffee, sending super
vague emails. It got so bad God personally had to speak to me.
This was annoying because I'm not a religious person. I thought
I'd made this clear to God by reading Harry Potter & not attending
church except for gay weddings. God did not listen to me. God is
not a good listener. I said Stop it please, I'll give you wedding cake,
money, candy, marijuana. Go talk to married people, politicians,
children, reality TV stars. I'll even set up a booth for you,
then everyone who wants to talk to you can do so
without the stuffy house of worship, the stuffier middlemen,
& the football blimps that accidentally intercept prayers
on their way to heaven. I'll keep the booth decorations simple
but attractive: stickers of angels & cats, because I'm not religious
but didn't people worship cats? Thing is, God couldn't take a hint.
My doctor said to eat an apple every day. My best friend said to stop
sleeping with guys with messiah complexes. My mother said she is
pretty sure she had sex with my father so I can't be some new
Asian Jesus. I tried to enrage God by saying things like When I asked
my mother about you, she was in the middle of making dinner
so she just said Too busy. I tried to confuse God by saying I am
a made-up dinosaur & a real dinosaur & who knows maybe
I love you, but then God ended up relating to me. God said I am
a good dinosaur but also sort of evil & sometimes loving no one.
It rained & we stayed inside. Played a few rounds of backgammon.
We used our indoor voices. It got so quiet I asked God
about the afterlife. Its existence, human continued existence.
He said Oh. That. Then sent his angel again. Who said Ummmmmmm.
I never heard from God or his rookie angel after that. I miss them.
Like creatures I made up or found in a book, then got to know a bit.

CLAUDIA EMERSON

Drybridge

1

Claude says he, too, was given the tracks and not
the train, the way – and not the way out, not the beyond
beyond that bend, or the next. The place

they call Drybridge – for the waterless bed
of rails – where, on the banks, you grow up learning
more news from hoboes than from the mailman.

But you know nothing of the train as it passes
behind the backs of grander houses, gutted

warehouses, chained dogs, as it grazes an alien
grid of fences – of stone, metal, and chain-link.
Or that when it passes beneath the underside

of a bridge, a boy your own age waves the way
you do, and that there is a horse doesn't lift its head,
and one that does, only to lower it again.

2

You are a grown man when the train comes
to a scalding stop, and a lantern swings down
the road. A man has been killed, they call out

from behind the light's aura, and would you come see
what you can tell of him by what's left. You do
know his hat, and that burn scar on the back

of his hand. What you know of his wife
you do not say and will not even the next

night when you sit up with the body in the house
he wanted that much shut of, her voice rigid
as its walls while the train you hear out there in the darkness

passes by the way it always does, as though
the same, the very same, and, again, on
the time it will this night be able to keep.

JOHN HENNESSY

Convenience Store Aquinas

7-Eleven's a misnomer, like "mind-
body" problem. They never close. The hyphen's

a dash of form. Sure, *this* mind-body's
a machine, if you want, plowing across town

to the steak house. American Spirit. Give us
the yellow pack. No matches? This dollar-

fifty-nine Santa lighter, too. Big Grab bag
of Doritos. No, the "engine" is not

separate – it's part of the machine. Sure, paper's
good, container for recycling. Rain's no problem.

I eat the Doritos, smoke up – one for you?
The chips are part of my machine –

matter inside matter – smoke fires my lungs,
gives me that slap of pleasure in my

tailbone, maybe stimulates a thought.
I'm prime matter informed by the soul.

No, I didn't just slip the word in there:
that's a spade – it digs through bullshit.

Lean close, under the awning, cover up,
you want a light. The mist can't decide

if it's rain or fog. Streetlight moons, clouds
around the neon signs. Pink as the steak

we're heading for. The comfort of a red leather
banquette. No, your engine exists as part of

and powers its machine; separated, both are just
scrap, bunch of gears, rusty sprockets.

An unlit oven. Unbaked potatoes. Sour cream
inside a cow, chives growing mostly underground.

"Engine" is a bad analogy. I'm one thing,
not two, no intermediaries. I don't

have a body, I am one. A hollow
one at the moment. What'll it be?

Filet mignon? Slab of prime rib, don't trim
the fat? Twelve oz. T-bone, two inches thick?

No, I'll wait until after I eat for another,
but you go right ahead. Here's a light.

AILISH HOPPER

Did It Ever Occur to You That Maybe You're Falling in Love?

We buried the problem.

We planted a tree over the problem.

We regretted our actions toward the problem.

We declined to comment on the problem.

We carved a memorial to the problem, dedicated it. Forgot our
handkerchief.

We removed all "unnatural" ingredients, handcrafted a locally-grown
tincture for the problem. But nobody bought it.

We freshly-laundered, bleached, deodorized the problem.

We built a wall around the problem, tagged it with pictures of children,
birds in trees.

We renamed the problem, and denounced those who used the old
name.

We wrote a law for the problem, but it died in committee.

We drove the problem out with loud noises from homemade
instruments.

We marched, leafleted, sang hymns, linked arms with the problem,
got dragged to jail, got spat on by the problem and let out.

We elected an official who Finally Gets the problem.

We raised an army to corral and question the problem. They went
door to door but could never ID.

We made www.problem.com so You Can Find Out About the
problem, and www.problem.org so You Can Help.

We created 1-800-Problem, so you could Report On the problem,
and 1-900-Problem so you could Be the Only Daddy That
Really Turns That problem On.

We drove the wheels offa that problem.

We rocked the shit out of that problem.

We amplified the problem, turned it on up, and blew it out.

We drank to forget the problem.

We inhaled the problem, exhaled the problem, crushed its ember
    under our shoe.
We put a title on the problem, took out all the articles, conjunctions,
    and verbs. Called it "Exprmntl Prblm."
We shot the problem, and put it out of its misery.
We swallowed daily pills for the problem, followed a problem fast,
    drank problem tea.
We read daily problem horoscopes. Had our problem palms read by
    a seer.
We prayed.
Burned problem incense.
Formed a problem task force. Got a problem degree. Got on the
    problem tenure track. Got a problem retirement plan.
We gutted and renovated the problem. We joined the
    Neighborhood Problem Development Corp.
We listened and communicated with the problem, only to find out
    that it had gone for the day.
We mutually empowered the problem.
We kissed and stroked the problem, we fucked the problem all night.
    Woke up to an empty bed.
We watched carefully for the problem, but our flashlight died.
We had dreams of the problem. In which we could no longer
    recognize ourselves.
We reformed. We transformed. Turned over a new leaf. Turned a
    corner, found ourselves near a scent that somehow reminded us
    of the problem,
In ways we could never
Put into words. That
Little I-can't-explain-it
That makes it hard to think. That
Rings like a siren inside.

CATE MARVIN

Dead Girl Gang Bang

Though I can't recall your last name
now, Howie, I've been penciling myself in
   to your way back then, way back
    when, in your gangbangland, she was
    loose and gone, struggling up on a limb
to raise herself off from your bed, but lost,
fell back, let the all of you in again. Said
  just trying to get out your room

was no use since she'd got her own
         self in. Curbside-mind, I venture
you are still alive. Wondering what she'd
         think of that, but, then, I don't
know, can a ghost think when its body's shot
  itself in the head? Hell, just thinking about
     it makes me wish I were dead. Just
some girl, you, then you letting your friends

shovel their coal-selves up into her, just some
    person. I knew. Her mother's now offering
      a twenty-percent discount for crystal
healing therapy on her website. In high school,
she was a calm mother, dull job as telephone
      operator, back in that town her dead
       daughter and I always swore we
would leave, back in that town dead to me,

    and me, I marry a man who mocks
    me for crying. *We-we-we*, he calls out,
snickering in the gloom. Yet still I wear the dead
    girl's perfume. And I've got an accident
     to report. Because it was all our centers,

uninvited, you rucked up inside, then bade your
friends park their reeking selves in the garage
      of her feminine. What did you call it

back then? You balding fuck, you've forgot.
  Sloppy seconds. Forgot her slippage, eyes dead
    drunk spirals, face some fluid spilling down
      your sheets. I've been where she's been,
and I can be where you are now, switch my hips,
sashay into your office to see you any day now,
    wearing her perfume. What pack animal
    would you choose to be in your next life?

    Every day, the marsupial clouds grow
  hungrier for our reunion, the reunion I've been
    packing for all my life. There is a swing set
and a girl in a dress who doesn't know about this
next. First, she's pretty. Finally, she's done for.
  So I took some pills to forget I knew you last
as friend. Then I learned the ways of your wiles,
    how you did my girl who's now dead in.

RICHARD O. MOORE

d e l e t e 12

Welcome to your day of sanity! Come in and close the door it will
likely lock behind you and you will be home alone waste disposal will
take care of your needs : at long last undisturbed phenomena without
the heavy metal background of the street will be yours for observation
and response : do you have visions? do you think? Your mouth
do you open it for more than medication? I should know I know that
I should know : we've watched centuries erode the fortress drain the
moat the poet's clumsy beast has reached its home and prey we wither
in the gridlock of our power only the guns remain and are in use
pure accident is beauty to be glimpsed your trembling only further
clouds your sight I in my home you in your other place harmonize
the fading anthem of an age the cracked bell of our liberty keeps time
a penny for the corpse you left behind keep on recycling all that you
have heard before call it a double bind much like the dead bolt that
locked the door that keeps you safe and sane : ho – hum – harry
who? oh that's just a phrase found in a time capsule capped and sealed
and shot up in the air : no I cannot tell you where it fell to earth that
page was torn out years ago it's chance that we have a fragment of that
language left : do your archaeology before a mirror the canyons and
the barren plains are clear but where to dig for a ruined golden age a
fiction we were served with breakfast flakes say have you forgot this
day of sanity? No problem the heavy key was thrown away as soon as
the door was closed and locked you're safe : some day the asylum may
be torn down to make way for a palace of the mad it does not follow
that anything will change : choose your executioner by lot almost
everyone is trained and competent there are different schools of
course check out degrees fees can become an issue of your choice and
some may be in service or abroad as usual nothing's simple it's all a
part of the grand unraveling that must take place before the new line
can be introduced : prepare now don't be shocked when the music
starts the year's fashions may feature pins and nails.

TOMÁS Q. MORÍN

Salad Days
for Micah Ruelle

We were not green in judgment or cold
in blood like Cleopatra in her youth
who still was ordering chopped radish
in her bowls back then,
the hearts all gone to pieces
next to the winter greens
that in our days we never had use for
so smitten were we with fire
and ovens that I was gravy in judgment,
which might not mean much
unless you've taken a spoon
of it and poured it back over a dumpling
shaped like your heart
so that it became even softer,
something you could not have thought possible.
It's all happening now,
you liked to say, and I agreed,
though it was not the news
from the outside I relished,
but the daily *Extra! Extra!* the light
of the morning brought to my attention
every time we woke in your house
or my house and my heart
– salty, risen – was warm
again in a way it hadn't been for years.
Organ of passion, organ of righteousness
that has never had a single flavor cross its lips,
how could you know
how much I would miss the honey of those days,
her drizzle of it on the turkey bacon,

my cracking pepper up and down the pan,
the sweet meat of happiness
I would no longer let pass between our teeth.

DONALD REVELL

Pericles

What are my friends? Mouths, not eyes for
Bitterest underflesh of the farewell.
I was a man and suffered like a girl.
I spoke underneath to where the lights are

Pretty, pretty, pretty whence they came to tell
One God gets another. My friends are
Mouths for God, tearing me. In such a world
Broken only daughter opens to splendor.

My first thought was that dying is a deep well
Into the image of death, a many of one girl.
Later it meant to smile with no face, where
Mirrors are mouths. Cupid and Psyche wore

Blindfolds made of glass, which explains why girls
Get to heaven early mornings Adam fell.
Gods after gods we go. Still later,
Friends shouldered high mountains to the lee shore.

Gashed, and the gash a fountain of waters,
The landscape defames a single flower:
Amaranth. Magic hides an island world
Of boys and one daughter. I buried a pearl

In God's eye. And yet He sees her,
Defames her, considers His time well
Spent imagining a continent of flowers
Whose final climate is a broken girl.

Bells of a Cretan woman in labor
Hurled from a tower, flesh realer
Than the ground she somehow upwards curled
Into the bloom of her groin where bells

Are bees. I am an old man with a new beard.
I am the offspring of my child sprung from hell.
Shipwreck makes peninsular metaphor
Out of my hatred, her rape, and one bell tower.

Confusion suicides the poems, heaven I heard
Where the juice runs from stone-struck flowers.
At the end of the world I must use proper
Violence. Nothing is more true to tell.

Tell the taut-strung higher calendars
I've a margent in mind and new words
Hope to say, catastrophe to hear,
Old confederates and inwood apples

Where apples never shone. Also tell
Of mountains shouldered underneath one flower
Called amaranth. They tired of the world
Who made the world this way. God never

Did, never will. If you were to call
From the bottom of the ocean, the words,
Every one to me a living daughter,
Would shout wild mercy as never was before.

ATSURO RILEY

Moth
– *Candy's Stop, up Hwy. 52*

I been 'Candy' since I came here young.

My born name keeps but I don't say.

To her who my mama was I was
pure millstone, cumbrance. *Child ain't but a towsack full of bane.*

Well I lit out right quick.

Hitched, and so forth. Legged it.
Was rid.

Accabee at first (then, thicket-hid) then Wadmalaw;
out to Nash's meat-yard, Obie's jook. At
County Home they had this jazzhorn drumbeat
orphan-band '*THEM LAMBS*' they –

They let me bide and listen.

This gristly man he came he buttered me
then took me off (swore I was surely something) let me ride in back.

Some *thing* –
(snared) (spat-on) Thing
being morelike moresoever what he meant.

No I'd never sound what brunts he called me what he done
had I a hundred mouths.

How his mouth. Repeats
on me down the years. Everlastingly
riveled-looking, like rotfruit. Wasn't it
runched up like a grub.

First chance I inched off (back through bindweed) I was gone.

Nothing wrong with *gone* as a place
for living. Whereby a spore eats air when she has to;
where I've fairly much clung for peace.

Came the day I came here young
I mothed
my self. I cleaved apart.

A soul can hide like moth on bark.
My born name keeps but I don't say.

CHRISTOPHER ROBLEY

Nano

Insects are small, they already know how to fly, and – best of all – they power
*   themselves.* – Emily Anthes

In an air-conditioned trailer, three geeks
barely beyond boyhood fist-bump and high-five

at a job well done. With the click of a key a dozen
soundless screens flutter. Now in the shallow

of a cave near the Khyber Pass, a stack of glow sticks
activated in the blast steeps the darkness green:

two cans of pineapple; a mangled can of beets
bleeding juice; some boy streaked black, his burns

wrapped in torn canvas tent flaps. He must hear the
cyborg beetle's brains buzz like a circuit-bent keyboard

above his Pashto prayers. But we know enough to
leave the live feed low, *audio is for the analysts.*

Our weapon : witnessing – : wired that way.
Somewhere in Texas or California or Kentucky

Taco Bell is on the table where too the kill list rests
quietly satisfied, and so its discord folds inward

like an origami acorn nestled sharply in the heart.

DANEZ SMITH

from *"summer, somewhere"*

sometimes a boy is born
right out the sky, dropped from

a bridge between starshine & clay.
one boy showed up pulled behind

a truck, a parade for himself
& his wet red gown. years ago

we plucked brothers from branches
unpeeled their naps from bark.

sometimes a boy walks into his room
then walks out into his new world

still clutching wicked metals. some boys
waded here through their own blood.

does it matter how he got here if we're all here
to dance? grab a boy, spin him around.

if he asks for a kiss, kiss him.
if he asks where he is, say gone.

    . . .

no need for geography
now that we're safe everywhere.

point to whatever you please
& call it church, home, or sweet love.

paradise is a world where everything
is a sanctuary & nothing is a gun.

here, if it grows it knows its place
in history. yesterday, a poplar

told me of old Forest
heavy with fruits I'd call uncle

bursting red pulp & set afire,
harvest of dark wind chimes.

after I fell from its limb
it kissed sap into my wound.

do you know what it's like to live
someplace that loves you back?

　　　. . .

here, everybody wanna be black & is.
look – the forest is a flock of boys

who never got to grow up, blooming
into forever, afros like maple crowns

reaching sap-slow toward sky. watch
Forest run in the rain, branches

melting into paper-soft curls, duck
under the mountain for shelter. watch

the mountain reveal itself a boy.
watch Mountain & Forest playing

in the rain, watch the rain melt everything
into a boy with brown eyes & wet naps –

the lake turns into a boy in the rain
the swamp – a boy in the rain

the fields of lavender – brothers
dancing between the storm.

      . . .

if you press your ear to the dirt
you can hear it hum, not like it's filled

with beetles & other low gods
but like a mouth rot with gospel

& other glories. listen to the dirt
crescendo a boy back.

come. celebrate. this
is everyday. every day

holy. everyday high
holiday. everyday new

year. every year, days get longer.
time clogged with boys. the boys

O the boys. they still come
in droves. the old world

keeps choking them. our new one
can't stop spitting them out

      . . .

ask the mountain-boy to put you on
his shoulders if you want to see

the old world, ask him for some lean
-in & you'll be home. step off him

& walk around your block.
grow wings & fly above your city.

all the guns fire toward heaven.
warning shots mince your feathers.

fall back to the metal-less side
of the mountain, cry if you need to.

that world of laws rendered us into dark
matter. we asked for nothing but our names

in a mouth we've known
for decades. some were blessed

to know the mouth.
our decades betrayed us.

      . . .

there, I drowned, back before, once.
there, I knew how to swim but couldn't.

there, men stood by shore & watched me blue.
there, I was a dead fish, the river's prince.

there, I had a face & then I didn't.
there, my mother cried over me

but I wasn't there. I was here, by my own
water, singing a song I learned somewhere

south of somewhere worse. that was when
direction mattered. now, everywhere

I am is the center of everything.
I must be the lord of something.

what was I before? a boy? a son?
a warning? a myth? I whistled

now I'm the God of whistling.
I built my Olympia downstream.

        . . .

you are not welcome here. trust
the trip will kill you. go home.

we earned this paradise
by a death we didn't deserve.

I am sure there are other heres.
a somewhere for every kind

of somebody, a heaven of brown
girls braiding on golden stoops

but here –

        how could I ever explain to you –

    someone prayed we'd rest in peace
    & here we are

    in peace   whole   all summer

KAREN SOLIE

Bitumen

One might understand Turner, you said, in North Atlantic sky
east-southeast from Newfoundland toward Hibernia.
Cloud darker than cloud cast doubt upon muttering, pacing water, even
backlit by a devouring glare that whitened its edges,
bent the bars. Waters apart from society by choice, their living room
the aftermath of accident or crime. When the storm comes,
we will see into it, there will be no near and no far. In sixty-five-foot seas
for the Ocean Ranger, green turned to black then white as molecules
changed places in the Jeanne d'Arc Basin, the way wood passes into
flame, and communication errors into catastrophic failure
for the Piper Alpha offshore from Aberdeen.

It burned freely. If I don't come home, is my house in order?
Big fear travels in the Sikorsky. Twelve-hour shifts travel with them,
the deluge system, aqueous foam. Machinery's one note
hammering the heart, identity compressed with intentions, drenched,
the tired body performs delicately timed, brutal tasks no training
adequately represents and which consume the perceivable world.
In beds on the drilling platform in suspended disbelief,
identified by the unlovely sea's aggression, no sleep aids,
should a directive come. Underwater welders deeply unconscious.
Survival suits profane in lockers. By dreams of marine flares
and inflatables, buoyant smoke, percolating fret,
one is weakened. Violence enters the imagination.

Clouds previously unrecorded. Unlocked, the gates of light
and technology of capture in bitumen oozing from fractures
in the earth or afloat like other fatty bodies, condensed
by sun and internal salts, harassing snakes with its fumes.
Light-sensitive bitumen of Judea upon which Joseph-Nicéphore Niépce
recorded the view from his bedroom. It looked nice. A new kind
of evidence developed from the camera obscura of experience

and memory, love-object to dote on and ignore. Collectible
photochrome postcards. Storm surge as weather segment,
tornadoes on YouTube relieve us of our boredom. In the rain,
drizzle, intermittent showers, unseasonable hurricane threatening
our flight plans, against a sea heaving photogenically,
straining at its chains like a monster in the flashbulbs, on wet stones
astonishingly slick, we take selfies, post them, and can't undo it.

Meaning takes place in time. By elevated circumstance
of Burtynsky's drone helicopters, revolutionary lenses
pester Alberta's tar sands, sulphur ponds' rhapsodic upturned faces,
photographs that happen in our name and in the name
of composition. Foreground entered at distance, the eye surveils
the McMurray Formation's freestanding ruin mid-aspect
to an infinity of abstraction. A physical symptom assails
our vocabulary and things acquire a literal feeling from which
one does not recover. Mineral dissolution, complete. Accommodation space,
low. Confinement, relatively broad, extremely complex stratigraphy,
reservoirs stacked and composite. An area roughly the size
of England stripped of boreal forest and muskeg, unburdened
by hydraulic rope shovels of its overburden. Humiliated,
blinded, walking in circles. Cycle of soak and dry and residue.

The will creates effects no will can overturn, and that seem,
with the passage of time, necessary, as the past assumes a pattern.
Thought approaches the future and the future,
like a heavy unconventional oil, advances. Hello infrastructure,
Dodge Ram 1500, no one else wants to get killed on Highway 63,
the all-weather road by the Wandering River where earthmovers remain
unmoved by our schedules. White crosses in the ditches,
white crosses in the glove box. The west stands for relocation, the east
for lost causes. Would you conspire to serve tourists in a fish restaurant
the rest of your life? I thought not. Drinks are on us bushpigs now,
though this camp is no place for a tradesman. Devon's Jackfish is five star,

an obvious exception. But McKenzie, Voyageur, Millennium, Borealis –
years ago we would have burned them to the ground. Suncor Firebag

has WiFi, but will track usage. Guard towers and turnstiles at Wapasu –
we're guests, after all, not prisoners, right?
Efficiently squalid, briskly producing raw sewage, black mold,
botulism, fleas, remorse, madness, lethargy, mud, it's not
a spiritual home, this bleach taste in the waterglass, layered garments,
fried food, bitter complaint in plywood drop-ceiling bedrooms strung out
on whatever and general offense and why doesn't anyone smoke
anymore. Dealers and prostitutes cultivate their terms
organically, as demand matures. The Athabasca River's color isn't good.
Should we not encourage a healthy dread of the wild places?
Consider the operator crushed by a slab of ice, our electrician mauled
by a bear at the front lines of project expansion
into the inhumane forest. Fear not, we are worth more than many sparrows.
They pay for insignificance with their lives. It's the structure.

Jackpine Mine photographs beautifully on the shoulders of the day,
in the minutes before sunset it's still legal to hunt. One might,
like Caspar David Friedrich's *Wanderer*, at a certain remove
from principal events, cut a sensitive figure in the presence
of the sublime. Except you can smell it down here. Corrosive
vapors unexpectedly distributed, caustic particulate infiltrates
your mood. As does the tar sands beetle whose bite scars, from whom
grown men run. Attracted by the same sorrowful chemical compound
emitted by damaged trees on which it feeds, its aural signature
approximates the rasp of causatum rubbing its parts together.
The only other living thing in situ, in the open pit where swims
the bitumen, extra brilliant, dense, massive, in the Greek *asphaltos*,
"to make stable," "to secure." Pharmacist's earth that resists decay,
resolves and attenuates, cleanses wounds. Once used to burn
the houses of our enemies, upgraded now to refinery-ready feedstock,
raw crude flowing through channels of production and distribution.

Combustion is our style. It steers all things from the black grave
of Athabasca-Wabiskaw. Cold Lake. Rail lines of

Lac-Mégantic. The optics are bad. We're all downstream now.
Action resembles waiting for a decision made
on our behalf, then despair after the fact. Despair which,
like bitumen itself, applied to render darker tones or an emphatic
tenebrism, imparts a velvety lustrous disposition,
but eventually discolors to a black treacle that degrades
any pigment it contacts. Details in sections of *Raft of the Medusa*
can no longer be discerned. In 1816, the *Medusa's* captain,
in a spasm of flamboyant incompetence, ran aground
on the African coast, and fearing the ire of his constituents,
refused to sacrifice the cannons. They turned on each other,
147 low souls herded onto a makeshift raft cut loose from lifeboats
of the wealthy and well-connected. The signs were there,

risk/reward coefficient alive in the wind, the locomotive,
small tragic towns left for work, where the only thing manufactured
is the need for work. Foreshortening and a receding horizon
include the viewer in the scene, should the viewer wish
to be included in the scene. One can't be sure if the brig, *Argus,*
is racing to the rescue or departing. It hesitates in the distance,
in its nimbus of fairer weather, the courage and compassion
of a new age onboard. Géricault's pyramidical composition –
dead and dying in the foreground from which the strong succeed upward
toward an emotional peak –
an influence for Turner's *Disaster at Sea*, the vortex structure of
The Slave Ship: all those abandoned, where is thy market now?

It's difficult to imagine everyone saved, it's unaffordable. Waves
disproportionate, organized in depth, panic modulating
the speaking voice. The situation so harshly primary and not beautiful
when you don't go to visit the seaside, but the seaside visits you,

rudely, breaks in through the basement, ascends stairs
to your bedroom, you can't think of it generally then. The constitution
of things is accustomed to hiding. Rearrangement will not suit us.
Certain low-lying river deltas. Island states, coastal regions –
floodwaters receding in measures like all we haven't seen the last of
reveal in stagnancies and bloat what's altered, as avernal exhalations
of mines and flares are altered but don't disappear. Still,
iceberg season is spectacular this year, worth the trip
to photograph in evening ourselves before the abundance when, aflame
in light that dissolves what it illuminates, water climbs
its own red walls, vermilion in the furnaces.

JAMILA WOODS

Daddy Dozens

My Daddy's forehead is so big, we don't need a dining room
table. My Daddy's forehead so big, his hat size is equator. So
big, it's a five-head. Tyra Banks burst into tears when she seen
my Daddy's forehead. My Daddy's forehead got its own area code.
My Daddy baseball cap got stretch marks. My Daddy pillowcase
got craters. His eyebrows need GPS to find each other. My Daddy
forehead lives in two time zones. Planets confuse my Daddy forehead
for the sun. Couch cushions lose quarters in the wrinkles in my Daddy
forehead. My Daddy so smart, he fall asleep with the movie on and
wake up soon as the credits start to roll. My Daddy so smart, he
perform surgery on his own ingrown toenail. Momma was not
impressed, but my Daddy got brains. My Daddy know exactly
how to drive me to my friend's house without lookin at no map.
My Daddy born here, he so smart, he know the highways like
the wrinkles in his forehead. He know the free clinics like the gray
hairs on his big ass head. My Daddy so smart, he wear a stethoscope
and a white coat. My Daddy drive to work in a minivan only slightly
bigger than his forehead, that's just how my Daddy rolls. My Daddy
got swag. My Daddy dance to 'Single Ladies' in the hallway.
My Daddy drink a small coffee cream and sugar. My Daddy
drink a whole can of Red Bull. My Daddy eat a whole pack
of sour Skittles and never had a cavity. My Daddy so smart,
he got a pullout couch in his office. Got a mini fridge there too.
Got a cell phone, and a pager, and a email address where I can leave
him messages when he's not at home. My Daddy's not home.
Momma saves a plate that turns cold.

But when my Daddy does come home, he got a office
in his bedroom too. Computer screen night light,
Momma says she can't sleep right, but my Daddy
got work, my Daddy at work, at home, in the attic,

with the TV on, in the dark, from the front yard,
through the windows, you can see him working, glass
flickering, my house got its own forehead, glinting, sweaty,
in the evening, while my Daddy at work, at home,

in his own area code,

a whole other time zone.

POETS READING

An occasional series in which poets write about their
current reading

. . .

Rebecca Perry on Bluets *by Maggie Nelson*

I first read *Bluets* in short bursts at the start of winter, on morning train journeys to work – partly above ground, rushing through the half-finished new builds of north London, and partly in the black tunnels and briefly orange stations of the city – cramped, hot, tired, noticing the faded blue of the seats. I read it again, from cover to cover, lying in bed on a grey morning. I looked up at my navy dressing gown, the turquoise towel hanging on the door, the North Pacific Ocean on the map above my bed reflecting in the mirror on the opposite wall and, very suddenly, the mid-January sky blue through the shreds of trees. Most recently, I studied it closely, one section at a time, in a bare office in Manchester, with rain hitting the windows. I happened to look at my phone – a friend had emailed, "I always pass this shocking brilliant blue near work. Now I think of flapping tarp", a reference to section 18 of the book:

A warm afternoon in early spring, New York City. We went to the Chelsea Hotel to fuck. Afterward, from the window of our room, I watched a blue tarp on a roof across the way flap in the wind. You slept, so it was my secret [...] It was the only time I came. It was essentially our lives. It was shaking.

She attached a photo of a large, blocky building, its black paint peeling in clumps, with an electric blue top floor. All of this is to testify: *Bluets* is a book that seeps blueness into your life.

Comprised of two hundred and forty prose sections, so interlinked that attempting to consider them in isolation feels like chipping a tile out of a mosaic, it is ostensibly a study of the author's abiding love of the colour blue. It has been called memoir, autobiography, lyric essay, poetry collection, bastard, hybrid. Frankly, it hardly seems to matter. The breadth of the book – encompassing history, philosophy, ichthyology, pain, loneliness, depression, shame, injury, solitude, confession, friendship, sex, and on and on – as well as the effortless mix of vernacular scholarship and stunning lyricism, blasts wide open any attempts at colouring by genre.

Section 1 begins, "Suppose I were to begin by saying that I had fallen in love with a color. Suppose I were to speak this as though it were a confession". This double "suppose" is the door through which we are allowed to enter. Immediately, the author requests something of us – that we take her at her word and follow, no questions asked. We enter into a transaction of sorts: a suppose in exchange for a confession. If we agree we get, in return, the chance to explore a many-roomed house, far deeper, higher and wider than the façade would have you believe.

In all of her dealings, Nelson is compelled to write right up to what she calls the "bad edge" of any topic. This tipping point in Nelson's writing is best considered in light of her manifesto for *Bluets*, stationed in section 62. It comes in retaliation to the 'Puritanism' of William Gass, who argues (in *On Being Blue: a Philosophical Inquiry*) contrary to the idea that readers want "the penetration of privacy... to see under the skirt." "What good is my peek at her pubic hair if I must also see the red lines made by her panties, the pimples on her rump... the stepped-on look of a day's-end muff?", he asks. Her answer is resounding:

For my part I have no interest in catching a glimpse of or offering you an unblemished ass or an airbrushed cunt. I am interested in having three orifices stuffed full of thick, veiny cock in the most unforgiving of poses and light.

Nelson is committed to exposing herself absolutely, honestly, on her own terms and at her invitation. The revelations we encounter are disarmingly open, self-flagellating and charming:

> I applied for grant after grant... describing how necessary my exploration of blue would be. In one application, written and sent late at night to a conservative Ivy League university, I described myself and my project as heathen, hedonistic and horny. I never got any funding.

Elswhere she writes, "Does the world look bluer from blue eyes? Probably not, but I choose to think so (self-aggrandizement)." There's no need to peek; she wouldn't let you look away.

In a *Bookslut* interview with Genevieve Hudson, Nelson speaks of the importance of the formulation set forth by Chris Kraus in her review of Eileen Myles's *Cool for You*. Kraus says, "Like [Kathy] Acker, Myles values the most intimate and 'shameful' details of her life not for what they tell her about herself but for what they tell us about the culture." In relation to Sir Thomas Browne's preoccupation with metempsychosis, or the transmigration of souls, Nelson has also spoken of "the wild and productive gambit" of leaning against other texts, histories, the lives of others – "a blurry unity" of consciousness. It is this commitment to the belief that individual experience transcends the personal, and to the criss-crossing of human experience, that lends *Bluets* a complexity and generosity unlike anything else I've read.

In looking backwards, Nelson reaches across the void of mere death, grabbing the hands of those others before her who also found themselves obsessed with colour, suffering or lost. As a result, *Bluets* feels busy, many-peopled, full to the top. We encounter Wittgenstein ("who wrote his *Remarks on Colour* during the last eighteen months of his life, while dying of stomach cancer"), Gertrude Stein (who "seems particularly worried about color and pain that seem to come from nowhere"), Goethe (who "was interested in the case of 'a lady who, after a fall by which an eye was bruised, saw all objects, but especially white objects, glittering in colours, even to an intolerable degree'"), Billie Holiday (who knew "that to see blue in deeper and deeper saturation is to move towards darkness"), female saints who gouge out their own eyes, Henry David Thoreau, Ralph Waldo Emerson, Marguerite Duras, Isaac Newton, and too many others to name. Spectres maybe, but ones that cast very real shadows on the pages, bridging the gaps between their lifetimes and ours.

In the realm of the present, Nelson leans on the prince of blue – the "you" of the book ("with the face of a derelict whose eyes literally leaked blue, and I called this one the prince of blue, which was, in fact, his name"), who leaves; and the princess of blue ("she has been, for almost two decades now, an excellent and primary supplier of blue") who remains, and her injured friend, never named. Section 22:

> [...] I had received a phone call. A friend had been in an accident. Perhaps she would not live. She had very little face, and her spine was broken in two places. She had not yet moved; the doctor described her as "a pebble in water."

It is in the sections that document this friendship, rather than in those that fixate on blue, or the princess or prince of blue (whose gaze Nelson seems often to avoid meeting) that the real heart of the book seems to lie:

> Over time my injured friend's feet have become blue and smooth from disuse. Their blue is the blue of skim milk [...] I think they look and feel very strange and beautiful. She does not agree. How could she – this is her body; its transformations, her grief.

Nelson describes the intense pain that her friend feels, that she cannot feel, as "an invisible jacket of burn between us". I think of this jacket of burn as the one tangible example of the "blurry unity" that Nelson seeks, and it is no coincidence that it appears to us in the form of fire, between these two people.

Assured in its grip but seeming always gentle, Nelson's is a confession that is taken hold of, pried open and inspected in detail ("Clearly I am not a private person, and quite possibly I am a fool"). It is a lesson in the multifarious, fascinating, compelling ways a person can write about one thing; though of course not about one thing at all – about almost everything.

Maggie Nelson, Bluets *(Wave Books, 2009).*

Dai George on Welsh poet John Ormond's Collected Poems

To immerse myself in John Ormond I've come back to Cardiff, one of three places where this chronically unsung poet can be read in situ. The other two are Dunvant, Ormond's hometown on the westernmost edge of the south Wales coalfield, and Tuscany, where in later life he wrote some of the least embarrassing English-language poetry about the *campagna* that you'll find:

> And each cloudless morning I climb up
> By the broken flagstone path where the vines,
> Pleating the mountainside together, make slow
> Melodies on its patient staves [...]
>
> ('Note from Cortona')

Born in 1923, this son of a village shoemaker could hymn the Italian landscape without any sense of being an impostor or middle-class bloat, precisely because (I'm tempted to suggest) he came to the middle class late. A newspaper reporter before he started on a celebrated career as an arts film maker, Ormond spearheaded a generation of bright working-class Welsh boys – yes, boys, by and large – who felt that their time had come. When you've grown up on a pit-town terrace, you don't fret about Tuscany sucking you in with clichés. You celebrate it as an unlikely victory and gift.

Before finding equanimity in foreign climes, Ormond had to wrestle with the thornier subject of where he grew up. As part of a poetic generation that came of age with the founding of *Poetry Wales* in 1965, Ormond defined the art of writing about south Wales realistically, sympathetically, unsparingly:

> Home was where the glacier long ago
> Gouged out the valley; where here
> And there the valley's sides cohered
> At bridges that had no grace [...]

We lived by one of them, a dingy
Ochre hasp over the branch railway.
Nearby the sidings stretched in smells
Of new pit-props leaking gold glue,
Of smoke and wild chives.

('Where Home Was')

It was a generation that traversed the tricky boundary between the prose impulse of social history and poetry's more musical offices. Dylan Thomas loomed large, both as dauntingly precocious elder brother and a warning of where too much music could lead. Ormond – who knew and loved Thomas – didn't always negotiate that post-Dylan borderline with perfect confidence, but at his finest he brought something strange and wonderful to the prosaic rhythms of the mid-century Anglo-Welsh identity poem: a film-maker's eye. Here's a passage from 'Full-Length Portrait of a Short Man', a character study of the bow-legged Valleys tailor Willy Bando:

His years were spent
Coaxing smooth drapes for praying shoulders
Humbled on soft-named farms, stitching Sunday-best
For the small Atlases who, six days every week,
Held up the owners' world in the colliery's
Wet headings.

If there's anything earnest or dowdy in this urge to bear witness to the coalfield, then it's undercut by the sweeping, cinematic montage, from "praying shoulders" on "soft-named farms" to "small Atlases" under "the colliery's / Wet headings". Ormond understood that real history, real portraiture, needs to achieve scale. It can't just shuffle forward through events, attempting modest realism; it requires the illusion of omniscience, stories told from middle distance.

His best-known poem also happens to be his greatest manipulation of scale. 'Cathedral Builders' begins:

They climbed on sketchy ladders towards God,
With winch and pulley hoisted hewn rock into heaven,
Inhabited sky with hammers, defied gravity,
Deified stone, took up God's house to meet him [...]

Taking the form of a single grand sentence folding outwards, verb to verb, the poem does beautiful justice to the labour and lives of these medieval masons, all the way to their final boast: "I bloody did that." At first it seems to be a triumph of linearity, an expertly managed sequence of clauses transporting us through time. However, after long reading, I've come to the conclusion that its brilliance rests on all the ways that it *subverts* linearity. Besides its long, synoptic time arc, you might say that the poem operates along a spatial vector of verticality: we're going up and down the ladders with the men, finding divinity in the heavens and the mundane, disappointing stuff of life below: the "suppers", "small beer" and "smelly wives" these workaday heroes (surely none too fragrant themselves) go home to every night.

'Cathedral Builders' is a commanding performance, so it's a particularly poignant irony that it should have become Ormond's greatest hit, when more often his poetic voice faltered, qualified, insisting on provisionality and doubt. We see this other side in the querulous title of 'Certain Questions for Monsieur Renoir', which was originally meant to be called, rather more imposingly, 'Blue Major' after Théophile Gauthier's 'Symphonie en Blanc Majeure'. While the poem luxuriates in vibrant, associative colour, riffing on the tonalities of blue in Renoir's *'La Parisienne'*, it's typical of Ormond's approach that this engagement comes, not via presumptuous ekphrasis, but an awkward one-sided dialogue. The speaker wonders where the blues of Renoir's palette began – perhaps "in blue / Of a sea-starwort?"

> Or in verdigris, perhaps,
> Blue on a Roman bead? Or in that regal blue
> Of the Phoenicians, of boiled whelks [...]

In the poem's deferential yet slightly needling tone, I hear the lingering, aspirant voice of the grammar-school boy who can't quite decide whether he feels entitled to high art, and still tries to talk up to it slightly – but with a delicious, countervailing desire to bring it down, to make a Roman bead share a pedestal with a boiled whelk. It's the same mixture of high and low, honour and irreverence, that we find among the cathedral builders.

Of his three main territories Ormond knew the Valleys best, writing about them as a fully mapped social space – albeit one he had a prodigal son's guilt about leaving behind. Italy he embraced with an openness that didn't have to second-guess itself. Cardiff, however, was where he lived and worked for most of his adult life, finding access to a wider world that stimulated his imagination even as it prompted hesitancy. It was in Cardiff that he encountered '*La Parisienne*' hanging in the National Museum of Wales. I imagine him in the Impressionists room with a notepad, perhaps a little squiffy at the tail end of a long lunch, jotting down his "certain questions" before pootling back up the Taff to his office at the BBC and another film about the art and landscapes he loved.

For eighteen years a plaque has adorned Ormond's family home on Conway Road, just around the corner from where I grew up. It's an unassuming tribute, now little visited it seems; one hopes that Seren's recent *Collected Poems* will surpass it, in time, as Ormond's monument. There's a special vanity or wishfulness involved in following a poet home – the more so, perhaps, when it also happens to be your home. Nevertheless, I don't think Ormond would have judged the impulse too harshly. 'Homing Pigeons' speaks about us humans "flying still", like the pigeons,

> And, despite awkwardness, being, as best we can,
> Committed, in the chance weather we approach,
> To what and where, without a sense of reward,
> We may reach and trust to be fed.

Each of those hedging, modest sub-clauses teaches me something about the art of poetry – how it's something achieved "despite awkwardness", in the teeth of "chance weather". But moreover this poem gives me courage to believe that there's a dignity in battling towards the final line, that glorious active clause, somewhere "We may reach and trust to be fed."

John Ormond, Collected Poems *(Seren, 2015).*

PASCALE PETIT

The Hummingbird Whisperer

Let the surgeon who opens my mother
be tender as a hummingbird whisperer.
Let him pull back the walls of her abdomen
and see uncut jewels under his knife.
Let him have a pet name for each part –
his hummers, oiseaux mouches,
his beija-flores, colibris, his almost
extinct hooded visorbearer.
Let him handle them with crystal instruments,
easing droppers down each throat
to check their stomach contents are rich
in micro insects and spider eggs,
the nectar of never-before-seen orchids.
Let him soothe them as their black eyes
turn to watch him. Let them be so calm he can
unwrap their dressings to measure their wings
and wipe blood from their feathers.
Let him clean each gorget and crest
so the colours shine with health.
Let my mother's dryads and sylphs,
hermits and Incas, her sapphires,
her ruby-topaz moustiques,
practise flying again – forwards, backwards,
on the spot, hovering and hyperactive
to the last in their silk compartments.
Let their dissolvable straitjackets
drop off at the appointed time. Let
the man who closes my mother's body
check that each flight feather is intact
and return her to the recovery room to land safely.

Musician-wren

My mother, who today is just
a coat hung on the line –

let me be a musician-wren
and nest in your pocket

to sing you these fluted notes
straight from the forest's throat.

CAROLINE BIRD

In These Days of Prohibition

Once the needle hits the record, it doesn't take much
more than a bottle and two chairs to make a speakeasy.
I am a ratified woman, there's no bulge in my bootleg.
I only ducked into this doorway to get out of the wet.

I know the cost of indiscretion, the tonsil-hit of ardent
spirits, the mobster-trucks that reach the coast, empty,
come back sloshing; the difference an evening makes.
Once the needle hits the record, it doesn't take much.

Purely out of interest, if we swilled but didn't swallow
would we circumvent the law? Cancel that order. Silly
question. It's a school night, plus personal liberty means
more than a bottle and two chairs in some speakeasy.

Sure, the Whiskey Rebellion's recruiting and who hasn't
hankered for rough moonshine, but mix the sunset with
glycerine and juniper berry, the dawn'll smell it on you.
Am I a ratified woman? Is that a bulge in your bootleg?

And even if, behind my ear, a magic button could revert
this whole place back into a billiard saloon, I'd still clink
in the basement of myself. I should go. This water tastes
strong. I ducked into this doorway to get *out* of the wet.

Go home to your chosen professional: your stoic nurse,
your abiding baker. Why thirst for untried concoctions?
Wordlessness erodes us and this bottle has no label; I'll
forget whom I belong to. Once the needle hits the record.

First Signs

It started in scraps like blue dandruff,
bruised snow. My brother came for tea
with a sky-flake on his nose.
After jogging, my trainers
smelt of aeroplane food.

I found a helium balloon stood upright
in my garden, string dangling, as if
trapped beneath a clear ceiling.
The sky-stones came next, pounding
the roof like severed heads,

a cloud smashed the greenhouse,
a turquoise flume gushed like angel vomit,
I was crying under my ravaged umbrella.
But then, quiet. I looked up
for the crack in the stratosphere. Nothing.

I hid in the cellar all day. My wife came home,
I was boarding up the skylight,
"What on earth are you doing?"
Her work clothes were dry.
That night I didn't dare rest: I saw atoms

in the air separating before me,
an invisible shattering, fistfuls of shivering
fragments camouflaged against their own fabric.
I knew the firmament could not sustain.
I scrunched my cold hand

around her sleeping palm, whispered
something she couldn't hear
about the chasm unravelling above,
the deluge gathering at its lip,
the leak, the hole in my head.

The Moment

It has rotated in my mind like a paper napkin
accidentally left in the pocket of a pair of jeans
in the washing machine

and now it's disintegrated into tiny flecks, and
these damn flecks are stuck to all my other thoughts,
like lint or glitter.

Some people have a phobia of glitter.
Maybe that's because it looks like
the disintegrated memory of *that* moment.

Perhaps I should have pickled it within my iris, just
revisited in dreams, but it's done now, scattered,
spun to pieces; I can't

reassemble the actual occurrence, or
think of anything else.

PATRICK MACKIE

Early Mandelstam

Tough little angels of sound are howling off the rich surfaces of the
    water tonight,
but do not let that worry you.
The river Avon is bright black and yet it is not worried.
Harsh little ripples of what is not in fact cold sweat lick and etch around
the edges as it goes bending and loosening downwards.
It is covered in fragments of speed moving in bright little twitches and
    gurgles.
All the sounds rush towards it as if they had just discovered thirst,
and then they skid off it because it is too dark to drink.
Its water is as suave and tough as a piano lid.
I have got the early Mandelstam blues bending in my brain.
The tunes are hard and quiet and permanent like the veins
stretched taut across the body of a small wet stone.
Mandelstam translated some of my best things into Russian a century
    or so ago,
and of course this was quite an honour for me,
though he should perhaps have waited for me to write them first.
It will just look like copying if I write them now.
The night-time is turning the day into a foreign language now,
a language that at least is equally foreign to us all,
one that breaks all the splendid syllables down into pieces
and then flings them over the pale buildings
as if description had been a bad idea in the first place.
The day is washing its face off in the wet black air.
Streetlights are wandering around on the vanishing slopes,
and getting older too seems to mean getting smaller and weirder by
    the day.
I have not been in an aeroplane for well over a decade,
and this is just a single example for you.
The revolution came and ate up all its poets as if they were merely
    sounds or moths

or starlight.
All the buildings here stand as still as ghosts that are frightened of
     themselves.
I am very slowly turning into water vapour.
I guess that it is one way of being
translated,
while the softness of the stone bridge still reaches and wavers like a tongue.

THOMAS McCARTHY

In a Fruit Cage

It's astonishing the way a passage of time has worked upon
This one last raspberry. The late surveyor-wasps of autumn, like me,

Test and measure with their thousand eyes the flesh
Of late aromatic fruit, this one red world of perishable

Goods, subjected now to a cool, fastidious measurement
Of insects, insects urgent with signals of survival –

In contrast to me, I must admit; myself less troubled
By what this globe of fleshly red contains; this wound

Of colour that stains us both inside my fruit cage. The
Hours, it seems, turn more slowly inside my own life, and

Fruit seems not a food at all, but something from art,
A bleeding metaphor, perhaps, of those fears and desires;

Of all the efforts of human will that insects lack, all the
Stained reticence of things that must, yet again, be cut back.

A Bedroom Window in Newfoundland

I sit here and think of a life less ordinary than an iceberg.
If only history were salt water and freezing temperatures
The entire 1st Newfoundland Regiment need never have
Sailed overseas to die in a war between silk fabric and
Silk fabric. It is so strange how the warm and powerful
Arrange so comfortably a culling of seals. Late snow clings
To the Narrows, an army assembles in the fishing rooms:
A fresh blizzard gathers courage in Avalon's immortal salt.

The Seven Pear Trees of Avigdor Arikha

Not rest, but arrest. This iron foundry
Where I work, this place they call art
Is where I slave in a frenzy of prayer.
If time covers me with the comfort of
An Anglo-Irish chinchilla rug
It is a vintage car not an armchair
That my unhappy arms now rest upon;
And if I seem merely a gorgeous
Throwback to another era in fine art,
It is not Samuel Beckett's fault
Or the fault of any man who stays
Awake, who cannot sleep with all
The fuss injustice makes.
Pastel and paint will pay for this in days

And days of busier furnaces offstage –
My incomparable grasp of the past
Is no more real than seven pears in a tree;
Nor can the fountain, pitcher, fruit, assuage
Acuity of vision in a Mogilev foundry.
This basket of iron fruit can't possibly last
As pears on glass, as transcendent dust.

PATRICK COTTER

War Games

So rare these days to come across
small boys playing at soldiers;
the mouthed sounds of bullets
in flight; the simulated gargles

of death and the choreographed
leap to the ground as if knocked
by shrapnel or gas. The field I pass
on a Sunday stroll is sprinkled

with little motley corpses. A few blend
with the colours of grass; with most
their blue, purple and teal tee-shirts
gleam like wounds in the landscape.

One has brought a sword
to the gunfight, but knowing
the smug old adage he announces
his sword is enchanted.

As to a wingless Saint Michael
the battlefield doffs its dead to him,
and they rise with a chuckle
after a light touch of his blade –

the bodies felled by plastic
Kalashnikovs, whose short
rapid barks ignite the magpies
in their grenade-round cores.

SUZANNAH EVANS

The Doomer's Daughter

I was raised with the knowledge that the worst could happen
on any given day. My schoolbag was weighted with extras:
iodine tablets, dynamo torch, distress flare.
My bedtime stories were from the SAS pocket survival guide
and school holidays were spent in an underground bunker
in Lincolnshire. He drilled the whole family every weekend
for the five kinds of apocalypse: nuclear, contagious,
climatic, super-intelligent, religious. I can put on a gas mask
and safe-suit in under sixty seconds, even with the light off.

When he died I realised there are kinds of disaster
that you cannot prepare yourself for. Still, I drive out
to our safe place every summer, sit on the locked grille
and imagine the provisions he'd gathered down there:
tins going slowly out of date in darkness,
beans in tomato sauce, peach halves in juice.

MATTHEW SWEENEY

Frogman

When the river rose as much as he hoped it would
and the first wavelets explored Kyrl's Quay,
he ran back up the hill to his house, unlocked
the heavy door, took the stairs two at a time, stood
on a chair to rummage on top of the wardrobe till
he got all of his diving suit that he'd secreted there.

Laying it on the bed, he admired it – not black, like
most suits, but dark green (ordered from Russia).
He undressed and got into the drysuit, checking
how he looked in the mirror. He strapped on the
backpack box and stuck his head in the diving mask.
The flippers he'd keep till he was entering the water.

Switching on the TV to see the progress of the flood,
he saw it was overrunning the city centre. Excellent,
he thought, locking the door and loping down the path.
His neighbour laughed loudly at the sight of him, but
he ignored the man, foregoing his usual greeting.
Minutes later the drivers couldn't look at the road.

Halfway across the Shaky Bridge, he donned his flippers,
hopped up on the parapet and dived in. Two boys
saw the splash and cheered. He swam on, rolling
over quickly to see the stream of bubbles in his wake.
He felt as lean in the water as a combat diver, maybe
he should have brought a knife and a limpet mine.

When he came to the bridge by the Gate cinema,
he had no need to climb out. No, he swam over the wall
and down the middle of North Main Street. Cars
were stalled, half-submerged. A young man splashed

alongside him, fully clothed and singing. Ahead,
a female Garda was attempting to direct the traffic.

He darted past her, alongside a pair of startled grilse.
Seagulls were circling overhead as he veered left
to Daunt Square where two men waded with a statue
of the Virgin, trying to get the flood to subside. Yeah!
The water was rising, soon it would be over the roofs.
He looked forward to being the city's last survivor.

The Red Helicopter

Who authorised the red helicopter
to fly over the city, and stay
buzzing there, cruising in wide
slow circles, like a giant vulture?

The noise crashed into my sleep
yesterday morning before I knew
what it was, then when I realised,
I looked out and saw nothing

though the blades kept whirring,
getting louder, then quieter, but
never stopping – they wouldn't until
they'd found what they were looking for.

I ducked under them to go into town
to buy the dinner. A cloud emptied
so I taxied home, and heard a search
was on for a sixty-three-year-old man.

I was that man but what had I done?
Had I killed someone and not noticed?
I went into the kitchen, played Coltrane
so loud it silenced the helicopter.

I also attacked the Scottish malt.
This morning the noise whacked me again,
so I ripped the shutters open, and
there it was, big and red in the sky.

It was hovering right above the house.
There was no hiding-place anymore.
I pulled on my kimono, marched out,
barefoot, onto the terrace, to stand there.

A.B. JACKSON

from *The Brendan Voyage*

The Coagulated Sea

The *Cog* spins northwards
       bucked by rough seas
her sails fully strained
       like hounds on short leash

Six unlucky brothers
       cough up their breakfast
their garments bibs
       indecorously splashed

The storm's holy force
       the waves' war zone
the crew turn ashen
       flesh weak on the bone

As winds fall a notch
       their spirits grow level
until a wraith of mist
       swallows their vessel

Brother to each brother
       looks insubstantial
a crew made of gauze
       a composite fog-animal

The *Cog* stops rocking
       and lies dead still
the sound of snapping twigs
       the work of some devil

Clicks or a 'tick-tock'
      the small voice of ice
coagulating waters
      moving at snail's pace

Brothers gaze in wonder
      ice plates or pancakes
flagstones and icebergs
      each with its own face

Mottled as mirror-glass
      or bubble-transparent
azure blue boulders
      a jewelled firmament

The *Cog* now encased
      it is Brendan who sees
a thin host ahead
      like spears or trees

To and fro swaying
      a multitude of masts
their hulls long crushed
      by glittering mouthparts

Dig, brothers, dig!
      with oars and kitchen knives
the crew hack and hammer
      their second skin of ice

They lever the boat loose
      like a tooth from a gum
Eastwards! turn east!
      cries trembling Brendan

The Walserands

We left that brilliant castle, those rich cornfields,
and cast off. Suddenly, from shore, unholy squeals
and creatures pursuing us with bows and arrows,
their bodies a hotchpotch of odd bedfellows:

long necks, like cranes, but their heads boar-heads;
wolves' teeth, human torsos, galloping dogs' legs.
"You there!" cried Brendan, "You hairy mixter-maxters!
Do you know God? Confess! You cannot catch us."

"Brendan," one grunted, "we knew Him, face to face:
as radiant angels we inhabited that high place.
When Lucifer dreamed and schemed we lay low,
said nothing; our punishment this freak show.

This gifted country is ours, an earthly paradise.
Our castle you know. Join us." Their piggy eyes
flashed, and in their native language they growled
something about food, something about gold.

The Sea Leaf

With calloused hands
        the monks row hard
their hearts mouse-hearts
        their minds glamoured

It is Brendan who cries
        and points north-east
a cricket-sized man
        afloat on a leaf

In his left hand a cup
        in his right hand a quill
the ocean his ink-pot
        his work cell

The quill is dipped
        then drip by drop
he fills to the brim
        his thimble-cup

Each full cup
        he tips and empties
Brendan he whispers
        I measure the seas

I measure the seas
        the crew sit pop-eyed
their faculties flipped
        and lightly fried

I measure the seas
        tara-loo tara-lay
by quill and by cup
        I'll finish by doomsday

Says Brendan O speck!
        you soft nugget!
this aim is a nonsense
        away and forget it

The tiny reply
        This world's wonders
are infinitely more
        than you and your brothers

A SPEAR IN THE SAND

Christopher Logue, War Music, *Faber, £20*
ISBN 9780571202188

reviewed by David Wheatley

. . .

What is the great heroic poem of our age? How about the *Iliad*, translated by (take your pick) Stanley Lombardo, Richmond Lattimore, Robert Fagles, Stephen Mitchell, Caroline Alexander or Alice Oswald? Suppose, though, I asked what the great anti-heroic poem of our age is? Also the *Iliad*, let me suggest, but this time in Christopher Logue's version, *War Music*. Writers on war poetry often enforce a distinction between the poetry of witness (World War I poetry) and the poetry of opinionation from a safe distance (Harold Pinter) with, most of the time, a degree of disapproval directed at the latter. Logue's masterwork is both of these things at once. The project began with a commission from the Third Programme in 1959 and was published in instalments from *Patrocleia* (1963) to *Cold Calls: War Music Continued* (2005), remaining unfinished at Logue's death in 2011. Readers of this edition who sniff opportunism in the helicopter on the dust jacket are mistaken: this has always been a topically opportunist poem. The young Logue served with the Black Watch and was posted to Palestine, where he was court-martialled and jailed: the comparison of Ajax, "grim underneath his tan", to Rommel at El Alamein is practically a "Shelley plain", as Browning might put it. But Logue is also very much a laureate of the first CND generation, of Ban the Bomb marches, and sixties protest poetry of the kind collected in his *Ode to the Dodo*. "I shall vote Labour because if I don't my balls will drop off", runs a typical line; it could be Logue's Thersites talking about Achilles round the camp-fire. The dead Patroclus inspires a knob-joke. Where is the "eminently noble" poet we were promised by Matthew Arnold?

An anti-heroic epic, then, "an *Iliad* rewritten by Thersites", as Claude Rawson has called *War Music*. Questions of seriousness versus flippancy will tend to centre on Logue's depiction of violence. In 'The *Iliad*, Poem of Force', Simone Weil characterises Homer's epic as the great poem of force: "force employed by man, force that enslaves man, force before which man's flesh shrinks away." The peculiar thing about Logue's handling of force is that it is often more graphic than Homer but more cartoonish at the same time. Here is the death of Lycon:

> His neck was cut clean through
> Except for a skein of flesh off which
> His head hung down like a melon.

No melon in Homer; "his head hung by the very skin", writes the greatest English translator of Homer, Chapman. Do we need the squishy afterthought? A good point of comparison here is that other sixties text of ultra-violence, Ted Hughes's *Crow*: "Her promises took off the top of his skull. [...] / His vows pulled out all her sinews." Sometimes it takes a heart of stone not to burst out laughing, as Wilde said of the death of Little Nell. There's not much mileage in accusing Logue (or Hughes) of a lack of subtlety when overstatement is the point, and not just on the battlefield. There is an amusing *Horrible Histories* sketch portraying the classical gods as a compensation racket for gullible humans ("Here at Gods Direct we have specialist Roman gods on hand twenty-four hours a day to review your petty, small-minded gripe"), and their portrayal in *War Music* is not so very different, with the racket run by a bunch of gangsters and their molls. Aphrodite calls Hera Zeus's "blubber-bummed wife with her gobstopper nipples", and Hera and Athene retaliate with chants of "Queen of the Foaming Hole".

Hera loves the Greeks and insists her husband support them too,

Aphrodite bats for the Trojans, and Apollo treats the whole business as a glorified Subbuteo game, getting a two-page spread of his name in mega-caps when he intervenes, in one of the poem's most dramatic passages, to kill Patroclus. When Joyce disembowels Gaelic myth in the Citizen chapter of *Ulysses*, the temptation is to assume that he is trampling on the original texts, whereas in reality the originals were already giddily satirical. Three hundred years before Logue, Pope's *Iliad* is full of bathos, while Erasmus found Homer's gods "full of folly", and so on all the way back to the unknowable source of Homer himself. While the gods flounce and pout, the sexual goings-on down below are fairly strong stuff. Achilles's epic sulk, lasting most of the book, is over the appropriation of his sex slave or prize "she", Briseis, by Agamemnon. Sexual injustice is when the wrong man enjoys the booty of war, not the sex slavery itself. The poetry is in the pitilessness.

Stylistically, *War Music* is a varied affair. Like *The Cantos*, it alternates between rolling verse paragraphs and jewelled fragments. Logue does battle scenes to match any Kurosawa film, often in long, loping lines, but keeps an *accelerando* effect at the ready for when the drama intensifies. But there is real weightiness here too, the weight of the world and the weight of the word. How much of an adjustment, I wonder, would be required before this battle scene from 'GBH' could be passed off as an offcut from Geoffrey Hill's own 'War Music':

> Impacted battle. Dust above a herd.
> Trachea, source of tears, sliced clean.
> Deckle-edged wounds: 'Poor Byfenapt, to know,' knocked clean
> Out of his armour like a half-set jelly,
> 'Your eyes to be still open yet not see,' or see
> A face split off,
> Sent skimming lidlike through the crunch
> Still smiling, but its pupils dots on dice.

The identity of 'Byfenapt' escapes me, but tinkerings with Homer's names and other anachronisms abound: an argument in heaven starts with George Solti bringing down his conductor's baton; Napoleon's cavalry officer Joachim Murat is ridiculed for packing "50 pots of facial mayonnaise" for battle; and the joy of combat is likened to that of an "Uzi shuddering warm against your hip". As in Pound's *Homage to Sextus*

Propertius, anachronism contributes to the anti-heroic mood, serving up a junk shop of broken images, fractured allusions, and knocked-off grandeur. It also helps smooth the connections between the "ineffable imbecility" of the two empires Pound had in mind in 1919, ancient Roman and contemporary British.

War Music was described by its author as an "account" of the original rather than a translation (Logue had no Greek), but in his notes we see him honouring the epic convention of prepared similes "to be kept in reserve for some appropriate moment that never came", as his expert editor, Christopher Reid, writes. They're not the only lacuna in the text. Logue omits the description of the shield of Achilles from Book 18, at which point readers may wish to call an intermission while they reread Auden's great poem on that subject. Despite taking several times longer over his text than the ten years of the Trojan war, Logue never got as far as the combat of Achilles and Hector and all that flows from that, as so memorably condensed into Michael Longley's sonnet 'Ceasefire'. *Desunt cetera*, as we say in Latin. Ezra Pound's posthumous cantos have amounted to a handsomely proportioned volume, but Logue's leftovers are sadly slim pickings.

Given those absences, the poem's structure as it now stands suffers from some lopsidedness: the opening forty pages, for instance, are largely devoted to a plague of insects in the Greek camp while Agamemnon and Achilles quarrel over Briseis. The descriptions of Troy awaiting attack, the back-and-forth between the Greek and Trojan camps, and the arguments in heaven are orchestrated as finely as any George Solti performance, and the skirmishes of 'All Day Permanent Red' are thrilling stuff, but nothing compares to the fourth section, 'War Music', in which first Patroclus is killed and then Achilles overcomes his battle-shyness, to predictably terrible effect.

The paradox of Logue's achievement is that *War Music* is one long anti-war satire, without his ever proving that protest poetry as we now understand that term formed any part of Homer's intention. All we are saying is give peace a chance, as Achilles and Priam don't say. Once again, I fall back on the idea of anachronism. Logue is someone who can bring to a Homeric battle scene the snarky outrage of someone posting a comment on Facebook, and to the rowing of a shower of puffed-up blokes the steely poise and permanence of a classical hexameter. The author's notes follow the same logic of promiscuous mixing, pointing us towards

Likewise Patroclus broke among the Trojans.
A set of zealous bones covered with flesh,
Finished with bronze, dipped in blood,
And the whole being inspired by ferocity.

—Kill them!

My sweet Patroclus,

—Kill them!

As many as you can,
For
Coming behind you in the dusk you felt
— What was it? — felt the darkness part and then

Who had been patient with you,
Struck.

From *Patrocleia* by Christopher Logue (London: Scorpion Press, 1962).
With thanks to Rosemary Hill

his precursor translators but also unexpected sources such as August Kleinzahler, Emily Dickinson, and a Jacques Brel song translated by Logue's wife, Rosemary Hill. Mention of Logue's precursors reminds me of the long tradition of one translator finishing off another's work: Chapman finished Marlowe's *Hero and Leander*, and Pope had dogsbodies to help him with his Homer. It's hard to say who could step into the Attic breach for Logue and steer this wonderful masterwork to completion. Better perhaps to ponder the note of beautiful mutability and transience on which the published text ends:

> And Achilles, shaken, says:
> 'I know I will not make old bones.'

> And laid his scourge against their racing flanks.

> Someone has left a spear stuck in the sand.

David Wheatley's latest collection is A Nest on the Waves *(Gallery, 2010).*

GHOSTS

Andrew Motion, Peace Talks, *Faber £14.99*
ISBN 9780571325474
Tracey Herd, Not In This World, *Bloodaxe, £9.95*
ISBN 9781852248949

reviewed by Kate Bingham

. . .

In April 2014, Andrew Motion and his radio producer flew to Germany to talk to the Desert Rats as they ended their last tour of duty in Afghanistan. The soldiers were reluctant to talk about the "bad things" they had seen, and Motion "felt the pressure of these unsaid things very strongly". Listening to the transcripts afterwards, he wrote on the Radio 4 blog, the "expressions that most interested me were in-between the sentences that I had heard spoken. They were implications, not bold utterances. The pity was in the pauses, the silences, the suppressions; the poetry, if there was to be any, had to catch these things, and not hunt for eloquence." The result won him the Ted Hughes Award for New Work in Poetry, and appears as 'Peace Talks' at the end of this generous new collection.

   Motion has been turning other people's words into poems for a while now, and writing about war and the legacy of war for even longer. Did the Desert Rats' *suppressions* remind him of his own father's reticence about the Second World War – an important theme in his previous two collections? Though full of questions "I never dare to ask", the Motion of 'Veteran' (from *The Cinder Path*) was heartbreakingly scrupulous:

> I would rather not show
> the appetite to know
>
> how much of his own self
> he shattered on my behalf.

Six years on, he is less delicate about "the silence my father had brought back with him / ten years before from Germany which now could not be ended / although the reason for that was one more thing he never gave" ('The Camp'):

> What else could there possibly be on earth for us to talk about
> that was more interesting than a blackbird calling in the hedge

In case you don't know, the answer lies in 'A Pine Cone' next-door, but the point is Motion's language: heavy with the bitter humour of a grimly unfunny family joke.

Even the most fortunate English children of the forties and fifties grew up surrounded by trauma, and behind the seemingly simple childhood poems that lead the first half of this book into its 'Laurels and Donkeys' second section, the fascination and respect young Motion feels for his father is mixed with dread. In their way, these too are poems about war, and more interesting than the pity-of-war work that follows. Like the compelling monologues of 'Peace Talks', many end with a kind of wish for obliteration or, in the mesmerised dreamy bed-time poem 'Wait', engulfing panic.

Motion's early-morning writing routine is well known. He says he believes in "the dream life", and by moving directly from pillow to paper hopes to preserve "a balance between the conscious and unconscious mind" (*Telegraph*, 2012). Perhaps this accounts for the cinematic adventures of 'A Fight in Poland', 'Swim', 'The Burning Car' and 'The Notary', which begin in flat reality but acquire through their telling a wider, almost allegorical resonance and authority. In another interview from 2012, (the *Hampstead & Highgate Express* this time – if nothing else, being former Poet Laureate guarantees a lifetime of publicity), envying his friend Larkin's "amazing access to himself", Motion confided "it's something I'm still trying to achieve." These open-textured, slightly unhinged poems suggest he's making good progress, and it can't be a coincidence that the strongest, 'The Fish in Australia', recalls so vividly Ted Hughes's famous description of access in 'Poetry in the Making': "That process of raid, or persuasion, or ambush, or dogged hunting, or surrender, is the kind of thinking we have to learn, and if we do not somehow learn it, then our minds lie in us like the fish in the pond of a man who cannot fish." Casting into "a perfect circle / of still and silent water"

> [...] like the lid
> of a tunnel piercing through
> the planet's fiery heart
> to the other side and England

the poet loses his hook to "something obstinate" on the bottom but defiantly – bravely – decides to keep fishing:

> and still cast out my line,
> my frail and useless lash,
> with no better reason now
> than to watch the thing lie down
> then lift and lie again,
> until such time arrives
> as the dark that swallowed up
> the sky has swallowed me.

Hughes is not the only ghost to speak through Motion in *Peace Talks*, and from Thoreau to Coleridge and Wordsworth to D.J. Enright via Keats, they grow less sure, and less protective perhaps, of their place in the world. Like the eponymous egg-laying mammal in 'An Echidna for Chris Wallace-Crabbe', they seem to understand

> that to start again at the beginning
> and change faster
> would only mean taking the straight road to extinction.

And in 'The Concern: Samuel Taylor Coleridge and William Wordsworth', the poets regret, ambiguously, "a painful idea / that our existence is of very little use". For all his public and private dedication to poetry, the only thing Motion seems certain of is that he will keep writing.

Tracey Herd seems to have been in doubt about even that during the fourteen years between her second and this third collection, *Not in This World*. You only have to read the back to discover it was inspired by living with clinical depression, and Herd is content, it seems, for readers to know that without the support of editors, friends, and Elizabeth Hartman, the book would have never been written. In contrast with this over-determined introduction, Hartman makes an elusive presiding spirit; already by 1987, the year she killed herself, her films were largely forgotten, and here she is upstaged by the likes of Norma Shearer and Joan Fontaine. Herd has a talent for dark dramatic monologues, so perhaps a few of the early first person narratives – 'The Little Sister', or 'Eyes Wide Shut', for instance – are in the voice of her muse, but with such a little-known muse it's hard to tell.

This is an unsettling collection. Against bleakly stylised fairytale landscapes of snowy frozen lakes and mirrored halls with chandeliers and champagne-laden banqueting tables, the poems emerge through flattened diction and painful or ugly emotion. Internal changes of tense and address make the tone of individual pieces hard to read, and though indisputably powerful, Herd's motifs refuse to cohere from poem to poem. Take roses, for instance. In 'The Imaginary Death of Star', where

> The audience throw roses
> onto the ice, soft toys, applause

they are an ironic fee paid by the prurient, but in 'Calling Card', written in memory of the American writer Marina Keegan, and the last poem in the book, their "bright, yellow buds" become sincerely offered words:

> I'll never be able to look at
> a yellow rose again
> without thinking of you

In 'Solo' they are the blood of cut wrists, in 'Ruffian' a racehorse is buried with "a solitary red rose", and in 'Olivia de Havilland' the poet wishes she could "create a rose, / a hybrid to bring you both together. But that would be too elaborate."

Herd is a risky writer who will not scruple to avoid a cliché, a rule-breaker unafraid of calling into question her own words. In 'Not James Dean', listing the names of dilapidated merry-go-round horses ("Trigger and Champion, / Silver and Blaze") she dares to comment "hardly poetry is it?", and the end of 'At the Captain's Table' asks

> How many ships have run aground
> on the rocks in the dark and storms.
> Who's counting? Who really cares?

Such recklessness is rare and admirable. Also, perhaps, self-destructive. These poems are not well-groomed, they don't look after themselves, or their readers either. Improvised from the numb snow-whiteness of depression into cruel dreams and the "bleak fairytales" of 'The Little Sister' ("She was pushed in front of a car. / I pray to God for my own salvation"), *Not in This World* is a challenging read. Even the "small moments of happiness" promised by its blurb are built on fantasy or dangerous innocence: the "plump, bountiful / landscape of snow" in 'What I Wanted' fosters a muffled silence, a world of

> [...] tracks that led off as far
> as a child's eye could see,
> and then a little further

And in 'What I remember', it's not the joy of winning a childhood running race that remains, but "feeling as if my heart would burst".

Kate Bingham's latest collection is Infragreen *(Seren, 2015).*

LYRIC SILHOUETTES

Linda Gregerson, Prodigal: New and Selected Poems
1976–2014, *Houghton Mifflin, $16.95*
ISBN 9780544301672
Marilyn Hacker, A Stranger's Mirror:
New and Selected Poems 1994–2014, *W.W. Norton, £29.95*
ISBN 9780393244649

reviewed by Tiffany Atkinson

. . .

As the saying almost goes, you wait years for a retrospective of a major US lyric poet, and then three come along at once. Linda Gregerson and Marilyn Hacker's respective *New and Selected* editions were published at the same time as the UK edition of the late Adrienne Rich's *Later Poems: Selected and New 1971–2012*. However coincidental this may be, it is tempting to read Hacker (b. 1942) and Gregerson (b. 1950) in the light of Rich's pioneering advances in the female lyric, both having amassed a body of work that articulates its shifts across the turn of the century.

Linda Gregerson's *Prodigal* compiles work from four collections written over almost forty years, and is prefaced by ten new poems; in *A Stranger's Mirror*, Marilyn Hacker, the more prolific poet, selects from four collections of the past twenty years and from her own translations of French and Francophone poets, opening the collection with twenty-five new poems.

The critical mass of their respective distinctions is impressive. Hacker's, for example, include the National Book Award, the Lambda Literary Award, the Lenore Marshall Poetry Prize, fellowships from the Guggenheim Foundation and the Ingram Merrill Foundation, and in 2008 she was made Chancellor of the Academy of American Poets. She is also an editor and prizewinning translator. Gregerson's include the American Academy of Arts and Letters Award, three Pushcart Prizes, and fellowships from the Guggenheim Foundation, the Mellon Foundation and the Rockefeller Foundation. She is also an established scholar of Renaissance literature, and holds a Professorship at the University of Michigan.

The intention of a *New and Selected* volume may be to introduce fresh readers to a poet by highlighting decisive moments in her oeuvre, but equally it may give longstanding readers the satisfaction of recognising the development of a characteristic poetic stride, however hard the new material may try to shake that off. In this respect, neither of these collections offers radical departures in the newer work, nor perhaps should they need to. Rather, they leave the reader with a sense of two distinct and unmistakable silhouettes in contemporary lyric poetry.

Hacker is famously transatlantic in her life and work, but she was a New Yorker before she was a Parisian, and the dexterity with which her trademark sonnets accommodate (as one critic put it) "lust and lunch" recalls Frank O'Hara as much as Rich, though the elasticity she develops between traditional form and urban, often polyglot lyric is entirely her own. It has been called radical for its treatment of lesbian love through the heteronormative format of the sonnet, but Hacker herself has resisted this attributing of an agenda to work which, as this collection testifies, is much more organic and diverse. The title poem, 'A Stranger's Mirror', is a sonnet crown that revisits several longstanding themes – desire, illness (especially of the female body), cityscapes and exile as seen now through an older, and estranged, rather than necessarily wiser, reflection. For the new reader it makes a good introduction to the selected work:

> There's not one story only, there are threads
> of consanguinity and contraband.
> A risk that is familiar and remote,
> in remembered streets, imagined beds,
> shrugs into its sleeves, extends a hand
> beside the bookshelves, in a borrowed coat.

But Hacker is also an excellent translator of Francophone Arabic poets, and a large proportion of the newer poems reflect her working knowledge of Middle Eastern stories, voices, politics and poetic forms – thus pantoums and ghazals jostle against renga, sapphics and sestinas. As always, Hacker's inhabiting of form feels integral to her thinking rather than a stylistic flourish or fashionable cultural gesture, or, as 'Fadwa: The Education of the Poet' puts it, "a stanza's a room; a single line in the house / you – you – can build, throw open the doors to your vision". Nonetheless, some forms just seem to sit more comfortably in English than others, and the repetition in a 'true' ghazal, for example, can sometimes sound a little leaden and callow, as in 'Tahrir':

Through the skein of years, I had nothing to fear from this place.
How final and brief it would be to disappear from this place.

The tangle of driftwood and Coke cans and kelp in the sand
made me think of the muddle that drove us (my dear) from this place.

And if a poet with Hacker's formal wizardry can't do the Anglophone ghazal justice, one can't help but wonder who can.

Nonetheless the new poems' explicit involvement with contemporary politics maintains Hacker's commitment to the unflinching probing of personal mortifications, while always keeping in the mind-of-the-poem the larger scourges of American and European history. Thus, of her own cancer treatment and mastectomy:

It's not Auschwitz. It's not the Vel d'Hiv.
It's not gang rape in Bosnia or
gang rape and gutting in El Salvador.
My self-betraying body needs to grieve
at how hatreds metastasize.
('Cancer Winter')

In such gestures the personal become a means of accessing the political, a form of activism and reflective connection.

Many of these poems are dedicated to friends and fellow-poets, and as such, together with frequent references to letters throughout – "Where's the 'you' to whom I might write a letter?" – give the work an epistolary quality, the letter being a format that mimics lyric's own mix of immediacy and premeditated composition. It also bespeaks a certain faith in language and 'slow' communication that seems almost nostalgic in a digital era: perhaps a poet who is also a translator learns to hold postmodern suspicions of the signifier at bay just long enough for contact to occur:

> Letter, then, to light, which is open-ended,
> folds, expands, but even on winter mornings
> faithfully attends to the correspondence,
> answers the question.
>
> ('*Lettera amorosa*')

While Hacker's distinctive poetic stride is the artfully marshalled logorrhoea of the iambic pentameter, Gregerson's verse is freer, but still tightly curated. Her habitual iambics are scored more for live utterance, broken up into breathier pitch-shifts, as in one of the new poems, 'Ceres Lamenting':

> Last night too – do all
> of our stories begin with rape? – the girl
>   came back
> from the dead somehow.

Gregerson has often remarked in interview that her characteristic wasp-waisted tercet allowed her to break from the left-aligned blocks of text that she felt became "airless", and indeed, this stanza form has a bounce that is almost gestural, reinforcing the intimacy-effect of speech:

>   What I
> remember is Oscar Nordby at eighty-
>
> nine, rinsing his eye in an eyecup.
>   It must
> have been – don't you think so? – the good
>
> eye, though from this distance I can't
>   be sure.
>
> ('Creation Myth')

For the measure of how different this lyric pitching is from Hacker's, here is Gregerson writing about illness:

> The body in health, the body in sickness,
> > inscribing
> > its versatile logic till the least
>
> of us must, willy-nilly, learn
> > to read.
> > And even in error, as when
>
> The mutant multiplies, or first
> > my right eye,
> now my left, is targeted
>
> for harm by the system
> > designed
> > to keep it safe,
>
> even in error the body
> > wields cunning
> > as birches in leaf wield light.
> > > ('The Bad Physician')

And here is Hacker, again from 'Cancer Winter':

> I woke up, and the surgeon said, "You're cured."
> Strapped to the gurney, in the cotton gown
> and pants I was wearing when they slid me down
> onto the table, made the straps secure
> while I stared at the hydra-headed O.R.
> lamp, I took in the tall, confident, brown-
> skinned man, and the ache I couldn't quite call pain
> from where my right breast wasn't anymore [...]

The apparent lightness and euphemism of Gregerson's lines ("till the least // of us must, willy-nilly, learn / to read") seem to suggest a certain stoicism and acceptance; yet against the flatlands, malls and suburban living-rooms of the American Midwest, *Prodigal* is shot through with illness, mental disturbance, environmental damage and, especially, a parent's anxiety (many poems are explicitly about parenting) over the brutalisation of children: "No matter part // of his mouth is missing, eyelid / torn, / the rest of his face such a mass // of infection and half-healed burns they'll / never / make it right again" ('Pass Over'). While not a poetry of activism, it is a poetry of conscience, a kind of parenting-at-large, very careful about where blame may be assigned: "No fault. / The fault's in nature, who will // without system or explanation / make permanent / havoc of little mistakes" ('An Arbor'). And while children are often idealised, almost idolised in the work – "the elegant economy with which God / sculpts / the infant face" ('Bunting'), it is also clear-eyed and acutely aware of its own potential self-deceptions. These tensions make for intelligent and unexpected swerves: describing the triumph of her young daughter, "whose / right hand and foot do not obey her" learning to ride a bike, Gregerson writes, "I knew / what it was like / to fly. Sentiment softens the bone in its socket. Half / the gorgeous light show we attribute to the setting sun / is atmospheric / trash. Joy is something else again, ask Megan / on her two bright wheels" ('Grammatical Mood'). In a world in which "The gods in their mercy [...] no longer seem // to take our troubles much / to heart" ('Font') such moments draw on a different American tradition, perhaps that of William Carlos Williams, able to wrest moments of uneasy transcendence from close attention, and the poems' scoring artfully shows the mercurial flux of the thought as it happens.

The range of this thought is prodigious, and the new poems in particular take on a Protean range of voices, from the Roman gods to Pythagoras. As with Hacker's work, there is little of the edgy linguistic paranoia or fixation on the surface effects of language that has come to characterise much contemporary poetry. Both poets treat language as a material that may be hammered and woven into sufficiently biddable shapes for the articulation of real world concerns, and their respective accolades will testify to the need for this. Neither is as confrontational as Rich, or as groundbreaking, but then, who is? Both books are significant compendia of a life's work that will reward devotees and new readers alike.

Tiffany Atkinson's third collection is So Many Moving Parts *(Bloodaxe, 2014).*

THE RESIDUAL SPIRITUAL

Maitreyabandhu, Yarn, *Bloodaxe, £9.95*
ISBN 9781780372624
John Glenday, The Golden Mean, *Picador, £9.99*
ISBN 9781447253914

reviewed by Ben Wilkinson

. . .

On the face of it, Matthew Arnold's prediction that poetry might one day replace religion looks as laughable as ever. But despite a faddish tendency towards the defensively sceptical and ironic, plenty of contemporary poetry retains an enduring spirituality that's difficult to ignore. Major voices like Don Paterson, Geoffrey Hill, John Burnside and Carol Ann Duffy are drawn to the numinous time and again – for differing reasons, but no doubt because poetry can serve as a bridge between the tangible and the mystical, the familiar ands the strange, between what we think we know and what, it turns out, we really don't. Metaphor-making and soul-searching, the best poems plug us back into a primal sense of unity, reinventing language to show us that everything is a part of everything else. Here, the spiritual is never more than a judicious line-break away.

Maitreyabandhu was born Ian Johnson, before receiving his given name after being ordained into a Buddhist Order. From the off, this might suggest his poetry is an acquired taste, attuned to a particular religious domain; he is also an advocate of 'mindfulness', a practice that encourages paying close attention to one's body, feelings and thoughts, presumably in an attempt to keep a hold on our manic present. But if this sounds like the kind of irritating verse that advances little more than a torpid sense of wellbeing, Maitreyabandhu is typically too interesting a writer to fall into that trap. For starters, his work is rarely prescriptive; and while the opening poem of this second collection, *Yarn*, is a rather mannered hymn to quiet attention paid and rewarded, the best of these poems speak as much of psychological harm, uncertainty and the divisions we create, as they do of unity, beauty, or well-adjusted contentment.

"He felt himself the painful intersection / between two blissful worlds", begins 'The Postulant', a haunting sonnet which offers a portrait of the speaker's divided psyche. Here, the desire to be welcomed into a religious order is located in the promise of relief from a certain state of mind: "his heaving breath / was chain-link or the figure of eight rotating". But if the most stimulating poems in *Yarn* are anything to go by, the struggle between two selves is one that can only ever be negotiated. It stands as an inevitability, to be met with self-reflection and personal resolve, just as the speaker in 'The Marker' finds, in the book of his life, an ominous bookmark ahead of his own. For some, an open-ended faith like Buddhism might offer a partial solution, as the poet suggests in 'The World of Senses', in which he praises "the Lotus Born" guru to deliver him from giddy sensation. But even here, the poem primarily maps the chasm between a fulfilling perspective brought about by mindful faith, and the instinctive pursuit of more gratifying pleasures, yearning for "this much-desired success / [...] that barely adds a farthing to my store".

Maitreyabandhu's verse challenges most when, with honesty and clarity, it looks at and thinks about that daily dilemma that we always need to pay more attention to: namely, how to balance our narrow ambitions and desires with a genuinely ethical, communal outlook. Or, as the preaching nomad in 'The Cattle Farmer's Tale' puts it to one well-off farm owner:

> 'There are two thoughts, Dhaniya,' –
> the vagrant laid his hand upon my arm –
> 'one leads to suffering, the other to joy.
> The first is yoked to yearning like a calf,
> a suckling calf that's yoked unto his mother,

the other's like a shadow that never parts.
That intoxicated man whose main delight
is in family, wealth and cattle, death
comes and carries him off like a great flood
that sweeps away a sleeping village – sons
are no protection, nor father's land, nor wife.'

This tale is one of three lengthy "yarns" that lend the book its title, exhibiting Maitreyabandhu's way with sustained storytelling. Whatever your taste for this kind of thing, it shows something of the possibilities of narrative verse where the more fashionable lyric mode can sometimes fall short. For one, the use of dialogue allows for a particular kind of moral instruction, as the poem makes up for what it lacks in single-minded complexity with its brand of spoken immediacy and easy profundity. Food for thought – and some of the lesser lyrics in *Yarn* look rather meagre alongside. A few draw on religious literature too heavily, sounding a pious note that can irritate (a fruit that is "plump with a holy Now" and grows "into an everlasting truth"), while others gesture towards imaginative transformation elsewhere, rather than working to conjure it within the language itself. In the end, though, the impression is of a poet who combines a self-effacing, observational stance with often searing, complicated feeling. Maitreyabandhu is capable of crafting lapidary poems, and ones that are as likely to see souls "turned to birds" and "transformed to deer" as they are to confront the reality of a past loved one's absence. "So what can I conclude on your departure?" asks the poet, "that nothing came of it, with everything, / *everything* undone?"

If *Yarn* is a collection where the transcendent promise of Buddhist enlightenment meets with the blunt reality of flawed humanity, John Glenday's fourth book of poems, *The Golden Mean*, continues the Scottish poet's attempts to unearth spiritual meaning from the rooted physicality of the muck and matter we call home. Or, at least, that elusive place we yearn to call home: "neighbouring and impossible, / that city neither of us has ever found", as 'Abaton' puts it, "luminous avenues of weather / gathering the cluttered light like window glass". Here is a poet of sombre hope, whose typically slight poems can be as potent as a single malt. 'How to Pray' is an unadorned summation of his *ars poetica*, and one that deserves quoting in full:

If you ever decide you want to find God
look for him in a ploughed field, not high

overhead, in the drift of the distant weather.
And if you ask me how you should pray

to a buried God, I would say press
your lips into the earth, weight your voice

with the silence of earth and root and seed
and pray that all your prayers may be stones.

This is Glenday at his best: lyrical yet plain-speaking, philosophical yet unshowy, blurring the unabashedly numinous with a rooted specificity that is, somehow, as universal as you could hope. It is the work, I dare say, of a poet who puts out a short book of short poems every decade, unlike almost every one of his contemporaries (with a few honourable exceptions). Patience isn't always a virtue, mind; but in Glenday's case, the glacial emergence of his lyrics seems a process well matched to their nature: careful and deliberate; delicate and robust. Were you so inclined, you could dismiss many of these miniature lyric studies – lessons in observation, and intelligence worn lightly – at their unassuming titles: 'Song for a Swift', 'The Coalfish', 'Windfall'. But rather than clamouring for it, each richly repays the attention brought to it: a swift transformed from noun to verb, a soul in flight; the mysterious coalfish like a "gutting knife lost overboard". Or the ineffable sensation of love, "an unravelling / against the dark", like a child waiting for a star to drop.

And yet, as the critic once quipped, the risk in any poetic economy is too much inflation or deflation. Some of Glenday's vignettes err too much on the side of pared-back minimalism, which makes his forays into (slightly) longer, more conversational forms welcome. A ventriloquised soliloquy from the trenches, 'The Big Push', is especially powerful, imbuing the past with the felt immediacy of the present. As such, *The Golden Mean* – that mysterious ratio omnipresent in nature, from the whorls of the pinecone to the spirals of a snail's shell – is an apt title for a collection that looks to reconnect us with the wholeness of the universe, buzzing beyond our retinas and fingertips. In 'A Pint of Light', the speaker squares his childhood wonder at overhearing his father mention his favourite drink against the dull fact of watching him, years later, "pour out / the disappointing truth". But the image persists, just as these poems transform the everyday while honouring it: "each note he sings / turns somehow into light and light and light". Glenday's keen awareness that it's we, rather than the world, who are the fragmented ones, sustains and enriches his poetry. If that isn't the business end of meaningful spirituality, I don't know what is.

Ben Wilkinson won the Northern Promise Award at the 2014 Northern Writers' Awards. He reviews for the Guardian *and the* TLS.

THROUGH THE SMALL WINDOW

Anne-Marie Fyfe, House of Small Absences, *Seren, £9.99*
ISBN 9781781722404
Mel Pryor, Small Nuclear Family, *Eyewear, £9.99*
ISBN 9781908998828
Kate Miller, The Observances, *Carcanet, £9.95*
ISBN 9781906188153

reviewed by Judy Brown

. . .

Anne-Marie Fyfe's *House of Small Absences* is unified by its prevailing mood: a "disconsolate fugue" of the *unheimlich* and the nervily unmoored. Fyfe creates a set of interlocking, often institutional, spaces which are never quite comfortable or comprehensible. Memory wobbles, loops or is re-written: speakers seek patterns and fail to find them. The collection flirts with the fantastic but often draws on half-familiar milieus: uneasy European meanderings, city heights, hotels, childhood holidays.

Fyfe rings inventive changes on this twilit state, where "There's the same curve in the road / but the arc seems smaller" ('Headland House'). Her details can be finely judged: "There's always a lone post-war ambulance / parked up at 'Rosgrove', awaiting the call" ('Pilgrimage'); an insomniac speaker remembers her puppy, attacked by wasps while she slept ('The Outer Provinces of Sleep'). Vehicles are quite often "lone" or "last": "a lone lost *traghetto* / rising and falling on its way to the glove market" ('Late Rooms'). Lists are deployed – often several to a poem. This can work well: "Out there: roadkill, poachers, gunlamps" in 'The Outer Provinces of Sleep', but on occasion the cataloguing can overwhelm. With a single feature, the effect is powerful (is that really just a floating log "far out by the dead lightship" in 'Post-Industrial'?). And in some of the short poems – almost sketches – the details work very hard to earn their keep (eg, 'Salmon Port' and 'Our Little Town').

All in all it's a very thingy world, a universe of objects that are often recalcitrant, misplaced or faulty. At times, the characters are eclipsed by all the stuff, and a pronoun may appear some way down a poem, deliberately uncommunicative about the identity of its owner ('Honey and Wild Locusts', '*Vergissmeinnicht*'). These people, whoever they are, rarely control the paraphernalia.

Indeterminacy studs the collection: "the perplexity / of fly papers" ('House of Small Absences'); "tentative banisters / against her confusion" ('*Vergissmeinnicht*'); "Put it down / to a dreamy miasma if you will" ('Ocean House'). Often people can't be sure what has happened ('The Red Aeroplane' and 'Ocean House' play a similar trick). Like the condemned man in 'Last Order', Fyfe balances uncertainty with extreme particularity, as if undertaking an enumerative spiritual exercise. This serves her thematic concerns (and it works especially well in 'Late Rooms') but specificity can become an end in itself (so many names, times, ages!). Though it's clearly a device, the complex loading of epithets ("trad[ing] gudgeon pin / gauge sizes in pre-take-off hangar talk" ('Where Are You Now, Amelia Earhart?')) occasionally tires, and one fewer adjective or verbal gesture would have worked just as well.

The book creates a memorably uneasy world and the sound of these litanies can mesmerise. My favourites were the poems that had an organising conceit to keep them moving and manage the elaboration. This was the case with 'No Second Acts', 'Nights at the Memory Palace' and 'The Museum of Might-Have-Been' – where, wittily, "artefacts are still donated by the hour".

. . .

There is a toughness and speed about Mel Pryor's writing which doesn't derive from *what* it says, particularly. The pleasures of *Small Nuclear Family*, her first collection, are not primarily the pleasures of narration (though the book evokes a world of animals, family and city life) but, rather, how much interest she generates at the level of the line.

Pryor is a witty phrase-maker (a London café sells "muscular croissants", she watches "the North Circular's six a.m. rotating load", and a fly is "fat as a truffle"). It's more than that though: her lively and astringent style, with its good verbs and spiky diction, gives her sentences a quiet vividness. At a wedding, "The sun forces its way though coloured glass" ('St Bride's') and the bride, not quite sure what she's got herself into, is "trying, / down fifteen centuries of aisle, to bridge / the acreage between them". In a fine poem which marries facial features (eye, nostril, mouth, pupil) with astronomy images, a drunk friend balances on a parapet:

> What would it have taken – a dropped star? – for you to fall?
> You held glass like faith and lived to hear the tale.
> ('Walking the River Tay')

Pryor's (often long) sentences are efficiently handled and she knows how to draw her reader swiftly into a poem. 'Overseas', in which a couple take a sickly newborn on a long trip abroad because "there was still so much for us to see", starts:

> After the long birth like an opera
> the baby, neckless, silent,
> lifted from blood-arced sheets
> and pumped into song by a sudden
> audience of six and a breathing machine,
> we took off to a foreign country [...]

The division of the book into two halves sheds light on the title. The second mainly comprises poems about (and often to) husband and children, though the celebration of marriage is judicious rather than rose-tinted. The first section is more varied, and here Pryor transforms and complicates her material. 'Overseas' perhaps links to 'Spring Birth', a tonally smart fable narrated by a husband watching his unconscious wife being delivered, by Caesarean, of a cuckoo. Here are animals (gorilla, mosquito, rats, fly, and a slighter sequence about a lost cat) and things that pre-date, or threaten, the coherence of family: a dead ex-boyfriend, a just-deceased father, a honeymoon that is a qualified success, the London bombings.

Even in her slighter work, Pryor has a graceful sense of what a poem can do (and how to end one). Her poems unify elegantly across linked image or sharply executed rhyme. Her structures are often satisfying: '*Rattus Rattus*' contrasts two dead rats, one seen by her as a horrified child in Hong Kong ("How brave the cat, / I thought, that conquered, put a stop to that"), one as a mother in England, who touches the dead rat's "immaculate scrap" of a paw, "like the baby's in the five month scan". 'Sighting seals on a beach in the Farne Islands' shows what she can do with a nature poem. Pryor's rhyming is smart and skilful ("DNA/sashay", and "pins/pathogens" made me smile): 'Walking the River Tay' really only uses one rhyme – and that bit of flash by no means out-dazzles its other pleasures.

Though Pryor writes well enough to entice me to read what she writes on any subject, the more tightly wound, ambitious pieces, which gave a twist to her material, offered more on repeated readings than those which (like 'The Swan Hellenic Cruise') make a virtue of their modest aspirations.

. . .

Kate Miller's elegant first collection, *The Observances*, concentrates hard on its defined field of vision. This book is artful in many senses of the word, including the obvious. *The Observances* contains poems in the voices of artists ('Against This Light' and 'Colour Beginnings') and about sculptures, with a satisfyingly hands-on awareness of the physicality of artists' materials: "a pan of cobalt – fire-bright, / smutted, greasy" ('Colour Beginnings').

It's interesting, too, how sensitivity to nature and the close-to allows for an 'I' which is also artificed, part of the scenery: as model in a life class, or staring through a window at the sea: "Take me, a woman at a window, how / do I look?" ('Stay'). It works the other way more often: in 'The Deposition', a ladder in an art gallery mirrors a ladder in a painting (presumably with that title), and the sequence about the Nereid Monument talks of an uncle's fondness for one of the stone girls: "That's how he always spoke of her – as real" ('Girl Running Still').

This conscious arrangement creates a fascinating tension between the self-forgetfulness of concentration and intense awareness of the reader or observer. The picnicker's handleless spoon, half-wedged in mud, is "holding the trees in its stare, / balancing us on its shell" ('Regarding a Cloud'). Taken to extremes, the knowing contracted verb forms frame the 'I' as doubly self-aware: "As a child, I'd fossick / at the beach or down the garden, / reluctant – family photos show – to pose" ('Promise').

Miller's observation is skilful and she knows when to play up the prettiness, and when to break the mood. However, it's the way she handles the poem as a whole that keeps me gripped. Her gestural confidence generally stands her in good stead in bringing her poems to an end: just a finger's touch on the tiller and they smoothly shift into dock:

> Nightfall on the longest day
> – it doesn't fall. Detaches,
> lifts the warmth away.
>
> ('Longest Day')

The sure-footed austerity of these poems and their mannered tone make for a thought-provoking combination. The slightly arch quality comes from an occasional archaic note or didacticism, an unashamedly luxurious vocabulary ("satined", "turtled"), numerous 'ofs', and some lavish gestures ("so even this poor ground is inexhaustible" ('Promise')). Another contrast was the way that Miller breaks her lines, displaying her words on the page, while the music often seems to fall with a beat whose regularity belies the visual variation.

Thoughtful ordering results in an increasing sense of intimacy as the collection progresses. In section 4, 'Enter the Sea', the speaker is more obviously entangled with others and the water encroaches, eventually pouring through poems of family and love and separation. Miller's icy ability to sketch feeling with very few strokes is apparent in 'The Shift' and 'At the Dew Pond, West Dale' (sisters and sons respectively). The collection ends not just with the falling weight of water but with an open door.

Judy Brown's second collection, Crowd Sensations, *is published by Seren.*

THE WORLD WITHOUT US

Joseph Massey, Illocality, *Wave Books, $18*
ISBN 9781940696157

reviewed by Justin Quinn

. . .

Joseph Massey writes next to nothing. The texts themselves use very
little ink. A lot of the poems have about twenty words and one poem
has just three words (eighteen characters in total). The longest poem, one
of the few that goes over one page, has one hundred and fourteen words.
Occasionally he eschews verbs and articles in provocative ways, making
the poems sound like excerpts from longer remarks. Some are flush left
but reach only a short distance towards the right-hand side of the margin.
In others Massey uses left indents, suggesting that the whiteness has taken
small bites out of the black text. His poems are barely on the page.

Within these tiny confines, he employs alliteration, assonance, near-
anagrams and half-rhyme (sometimes stretching over brief phrases, not
only single words). Rhyme implies a traditional use of form, but Massey
comes out of a free-verse tradition that looks back to Lorine Niedecker
and William Carlos Williams (with occasional allusive nods to others). A
lot of the time he uses these devices so densely that the reader loses focus
on the objects or processes described, and attends instead to the way the
words themselves relate to each other – mirroring, echoing, one unfolding

out of the last, slotting back in again, allowing themselves to be mistaken for others. "Even a shade as it erases / radiates." Does this (as an older critical dispensation had it) enact what it describes? I can't tell, as I'm too entranced by the compressed verbal play to hold the sentence's meaning for long in my concentration. Page after page provides similar pleasures, and one realises that his minimalism allows words themselves to come forth in new ways, like workhorses happily unhitched from their harnesses, no longer obliged to convey human meaning from one place to another.

Then the true conundrum of Massey's poetry emerges: these are poems that are strikingly realistic. That is, they convey scenes, the kind of thing that might be seen by someone who (like Massey) lives in rural Massachusetts. Snow and ice give way in spring to slush and stained floes; this is perhaps viewed beyond an empty lot in a small town; a television might be flickering in a room, which mimics motions of light elsewhere in the scene. It is a world almost devoid of human action, though Massey does describe the small incursions of human making (that TV's light, signage calligraphy in neon or paint, edges and corners of concrete, fencing, metal frames, etc.). How could his words do the old work of description when they draw so much attention to themselves?

With carefully placed enjambments and shifts of semantic meaning, Massey wonders about this himself, or rather lets his words do the wondering:

> Apprehended
> by vision, we
> think we've seen.

> ('Take Place')

This tercet can be turned in several directions, all delicately disruptive of the way that humans see stories and meanings in the physical world around them. Time and again, Massey's poems show up as coincidence the collisions of language, and our thought, with the world. We *think* we've seen something, but really we've only been considering ourselves and our self-made visions. Or, we've seen something, but cannot be sure what. Regardless, we apprehend objects and imagine they reveal themselves to us. "Apprehended" suggests the violence of arrest, and also hints more generally at acts of grasping and seizing. In 'Notes Toward a Supreme Fiction', Wallace Stevens tells us that we should discover – not impose –

meaning. Massey shows this to be an almost impossible endeavour.

He makes this point in words, and this is a further facet of the conundrum above. It also suggests that these poems are a true manifestation of that fabled beast, anti-poetic poetry. Certainly many of the aspects mentioned above bring it close to this status. Moreover, the poems have a kind of implosive, centripetal force that makes it hard to imagine that Massey, continuing in this mode, would be able to articulate the poems into larger structures. Although there are sequences here, these have little formal integrity and fail to accumulate force – the real unit of the book is the single poem. Indeed, it is difficult to distinguish the poems in this book from those of his previous collection, *To Keep Time* (2014). Where can he go with such minimalist annotations of the physical world?

Perhaps this is a natural end. Perhaps he will only write further near-nonexistent texts about the changing seasons in the Pioneer Valley, much in the same mode as these. So committed to narratives of development, maturity and extension when considering artistic careers, we often fail to realise how useless these can be as a mode of understanding great achievements. Certainly, repetition can send the creative imagination, and consequently the reader, to sleep. It is dismaying to see poets repeating the effects for which they won some fame early in their careers. But that does not invalidate repetition as an artistic trajectory; a poet like Massey invites us to think in other ways about how art, and poems, might work in our lives. I for one will be happy to pick up such a book on any morning and read its poems again, and the next day after that.

Justin Quinn's most recent collection is Early House *(Gallery, 2015). He lives in Prague.*

NORTHERN EXPOSURE

Tim Cresswell, Fence, *Penned in the Margins, £9.99*
ISBN 9781908058317
Nancy Campbell, Disko Bay, *Enitharmon, £9.99*
ISBN 9781910392188

reviewed by A.B. Jackson

. . .

In his 1994 book *Enduring Dreams: An Exploration of Arctic Landscape*, Canadian author John Moss proposes: "The Arctic of outsiders is a landscape of the mind, shaped more in the imagination by reading than by experience and perception [...] Conventions of the text precede, determining how the wilderness is read; limits of narrative become the boundaries of landscape, and grammar topography." Expanding on this train of thought, he suggests that "[if] all the world's a text, then everything we know and do is intertextual". Writers travelling to the polar regions have little option, it seems, but to establish a relationship with the textual accounts of their forerunners before they can stake a little textual claim of their own, and Tim Cresswell is no different. Inspired by a two-week sailing trip around Svalbard on the schooner *Noorderlicht*, he alternates between poems based on personal experience of that Arctic environment and found poems constructed from the historical narratives of others.

It is language, more than landscape, that lies at the forefront of Cresswell's concerns, and the following extracts will give a sense of his signature style:

> from the middle English *fens*
> from the Old French *defense*
> from the Latin *defendere*
> to protect or defend
> as in *defence*
>
> > > *(from xvii)*

> the Dutch called whale oil
> > train oil
> from the Dutch word *traan*
> meaning *tear*
> > or *drop*
>
> > > *(from xxviii)*

> other names for the Bowhead include
> > *Balaena mysticetus*
> > *Arctic Right Whale*
> > *Greenland Right Whale*
> they were the 'right' whales to kill
>
> > > *(from xxxii)*

> and this spot   Gravneset
> which means 'grave site'
>
> > > *(from xi)*

Readers hoping for an immersive account of a life-changing Arctic adventure are treated instead to an awful amount of mansplaining, and the sort of information that can be gleaned from Wikipedia at a comfortable southern latitude from the safety of one's slippers. Cresswell doesn't say whether he saw any whales – perhaps he was unlucky. With regard to Svalbard's wide range of flora and fauna, he describes personal encounters with "skua" and "moss".

For the broader strokes, Cresswell prefers to employ Léonie d'Aunet's account of her travels to the archipelago in 1838, later published as

Voyage d'une femme au Spitzberg, and presumably translated by Cresswell himself. He follows her extended journey from Paris to Spitsbergen via Holland, Germany, Denmark and Norway; thus we learn, in her newly-edited words, that "Amsterdam is still a gay city" and "Hamburg is delightfully located between / the sea and hills covered with fertile plains". Finally, in the high north, icebergs are described in the time-honoured fashion of visual association: "a column copies / a huge table   a tower mimics / a staircase   bell towers   minarets / arches   pyramids / turrets domes / niches   scrolls / arcades   pediments [etc.]". Cresswell's second main source of found material is Robert Fotherby's account of his 1613 journey to the islands under the command of William Baffin, and this produces a memorable insight into the early whaling missions as recorded in the language of the day (albeit with modernised spelling):

> cut off his head – containing tongue and teeth – tow it to the
> shore till high tide – haul it up with crabs and capstowes –
> wait for low tide – cut out teeth with hatchets – four or six
> at once – lug further ashore – severed [sic] each one from each
> – scrape off the pitch from the ends of the teeth – with such
> scraping irons as coopers use [...]
> *(from* xliii)

It's not clear why Cresswell has chosen to refer to whales' "teeth" in this poem, or why he's introduced the odd image of scraping "pitch" off them, when Fotherby's 1613 original refers to whales' fins: "men maie come to cutt out the finnes, which thing they doe with hatchets, by 5 or 6 finnes at once [...] [They] scrapeth off the white pithie substance that is upon the roots or great ends of the finnes, with such scraping irons as coopers use."

In his original material, Cresswell sometimes comes unstuck in the summary details. In reference to the town of Longyearbyen, he states that "we arrived at the northernmost airport / [...] strolled the northernmost settlement / with over a thousand souls / [...] sent postcards from the northernmost post office". The northernmost settlement on Svalbard is not Longyearbyen, however, but Ny-Ålesund (also home to the northernmost airport and the northernmost post office). This list of unreliable touristy information does nothing to convey what Longyearbyen is actually like, in terms of its landscape or infrastructure, nor any of its rich history. Beyond all the intertextual corseting and etymological padding, Svalbard remains distant and undefined. Stretching two weeks of travel into a full-length collection is a tough assignment; it looks over-stretched in this instance.

Svalbard has no indigenous population: transient whalers and miners have been coming and going for centuries, following the work, as international scientists and tour operators now follow their own commitments. In choosing Greenland as the Arctic focus of her first collection, *Disko Bay*, Nancy Campbell is encountering – and representing – the Greenlandic Inuit who account for ninety per cent of the population. The majority of the poems are informed by Campbell's various residencies there; her genuine passion for the place and its culture is clear.

In the translations of traditional songs, we get a sense of that culture and its shamanistic inheritance: "There's only one way to kill your enemy: // You must bite my clit off, pull it inside out, / and use it as an arrowhead." Placing the Inuit-language originals at the head of these poems gives the language its due (the lines quoted are from a song beginning "Uvijera kiillugu mikkissavan!"). In the vast majority of *Disko Bay*, however, it is not clear whether Campbell is presenting English reworkings of traditional Greenlandic material or creating entirely original stories in what might be called the same spirit. The book's first section is dominated by narratives of hunting and folklore in which 'we' is used to voice the point of view of native people; the second section in the book, 'Ruin Island', revolves around "the legendary leader Qujaavaarssuk", as the cover note describes him, but there is no additional information which places this figure in his cultural or historical context. It is difficult, therefore, to know how to read this type of mythopoesis – are we encountering Inuit culture through an anglophone prism, or a yarn of the poet's own invention, or a mixture of both? Some poems contain an appealing, austere lyricism ("Below the dark cliffs, the wide water / below the wide water, the black seal / within the black seal, the red fish") while others veer too far towards a kind of impersonal folk-utterance and, as a consequence, come across as rather disembodied and unaffecting. When Campbell locates the action squarely in her home environment, as in the later poem 'Legends' – "Bexhill, I think it was, a brooding town, / bitter as a fag-end between the lips" – the result is much more convincing and engaging.

With the exception of one poem – 'Alagassaq / The Lesson' – Campbell does not openly reveal her own interactions with this foreign culture. Unlike the poems in Al Purdy's 1967 collection *North of Summer* for example, in which he recounts his sojourn with the Inuit of Baffin Island from the point of view of the perplexed outsider, she chooses not to represent herself. It is a notable and in some ways unfortunate omission: the aforementioned 'Alagassaq / The Lesson' is one of the best poems in this collection precisely because the author's subjective presence is registered. Trying to learn the native language,

> My echo of his welcome is grotesque.
> He laughs, an exorcism of *guillemets*,
> dark flocks of sound I'll never net, or say.

Those *guillemets* or quotation-marks are close enough to guillemots to add a little unexpected magic to those lines. Likewise, 'Oqqersuut / The Message', which addresses a loved one back in Britain, has the stamp of truth about it and is skilfully done.

Campbell makes use of traditional forms – there are four sonnets, three villanelles and one sestina in the first section of the book – and her sense of rhythm isn't always secure in the stressed ballad-type poems. No doubt the intention is to suggest the cross-cultural significance of song in the oral tradition, but the impact is weakened when the footing is uncertain. Like Cresswell, she also uses found material from historical sources. Taking various words from the glossary in *The Arctic Whaling Journals of William Scoresby the Younger Volume I* edited by C. Ian Jackson (though Campbell fails to acknowledge this source in her notes), nineteenth-century sailing terms are transformed into a spellbound love poem:

> my darklight, I bottlenose you
>
> my flat-aback, I fid you
>
> my fox, I careen you
>
> my galliot, I junk you
>
> my lipper, I mallemuch you
>
> my piggin, I chop you

In some cases, nouns have been reinvented as verbs ("fid": "a conical pin of hard wood"), while some terms – "flat-aback", "lipper" – gain wonderfully sensual connotations by virtue of their new context.

It may be a type of modesty on Campbell's part to devote so much of her attention to Greenlandic narratives and so little to her own encounter-narrative, an attempt to foreground the significance of the one at the expense of the other. Poets are free to exclude the autobiographical first person for whatever reasons they wish, of course. In the end, however, the act of ventriloquising Inuit culture in poems which reconstitute its content is fraught with issues of authenticity and intent, and Campbell's best poems are the ones written from her own, temperate viewpoint.

A.B. Jackson *sailed round Svalbard on the tall ship* Antigua *in June 2015. His second collection,* The Wilderness Party, *is published by Bloodaxe.*

U.S. AND US

The Best American Poetry 2015, *edited by Sherman Alexie*
Simon & Schuster, $18.99
ISBN 9781476708201
The Best British Poetry 2015, *edited by Emily Berry*
Salt, £9.99
ISBN 9781784630300

reviewed by Fiona Moore

. . .

Both editors make the necessary disclaimer: 'best' is subjective. The Salt *Best*, in its fifth year, feels like a poetry institution, though is still young compared to its American model, which has been going since 1988. This year's *Best American* editor, Sherman Alexie, in an entertaining introduction laying open the role's pitfalls, does his own audit of the contents: around sixty per cent female, forty per cent poets of colour... and at least seventy-five per cent professors, a self-confessed failure to find more poets outside the academy.

Qualitative judgements are harder to make. Each anthology contains over seventy poems chosen from magazines and organised alphabetically. The reading-for-review experience was like walking through an Italian street market years ago, along a straight cobbled road that stretched as far as the eye could see into rainy distance: a mixture of confusion (so much to look at) and excitement (what would come next?).

An immediately noticeable thing about *Best American* is that some poems contain a formal element; around twenty per cent says Alexie, who himself uses form. There is rhyme and there are stanzas, especially couplets. There are even (variedly) rhyming couplets; the book opens with Sarah Arvio's 'Bodhisattva':

> Oh my bodhisattva of new roses
> you've saved me from my no-love neurosis
>
> You've saved my old body from the fatwa
> Let's lie down in a bed of roses

That's from the popular Poem-a-Day website, most-used source in this year's *Best*. Alexie has read widely to broaden his catchment. Many poems make the personal and everyday strange but even the outright surreal ones tend to have some sort of associative thread. There are few straightforwardly narrative poems, few Americanly long ones and plenty of short lyrics whose tone is often sharply humorous, bemused. There's less of a feeling of largeness of scope than a bout of American browsing usually gives.

On first reading I wanted more names whose work excites me, marker trees in the American forest: D.A. Powell, Brenda Shaughnessy, Tracy K. Smith, Jason Schneiderman. But then there might not have been space for the discovery of poems by Chana Bloch, Danielle DeTiberus, Jamaal May and Monica Youn, last in the book, whose 'March of the Hanged Men' starts:

> 1.
>
> hyperarticulated giant black ants endlessly boiling out of a heaped-
> up hole in the sand
>
> 2.
>
> such a flow of any other thing would mean abundance but these ants
> replay a tape-loop vision

Each poet is allowed space at the back to discuss the poem; Youn's is loosely based on François Villon's 'Ballad of the Hanged Men'. Her note enhances the reading. In both books, some notes over-explain and risk deflating the reader. Others are so interesting and well written that they risk overshadowing their poem.

Youn's poem stretched my mental map of poetry; I'd have liked more of those. Claudia Rankine is present with an extract from *Citizen*. Other names well known in the UK include Louise Glück, Jane Hirshfield and Charles Simic.

Racial politics are addressed in several poems, including those by Terrance Hayes, Candace G. Wiley, and Jericho Brown in 'Homeland', which sort of takes place on a plane journey:

> [...] In America that year, black people kept dreaming
> That the president got shot. Then the president got shot
>
> Breaking into the White House. He claimed to have lost
> His keys. What's the proper name for a man caught stealing
>
> Into his own home? I asked a few passengers.

(Issues of race entered *Best American* another way: Alexie chose a poem by a white man who'd assumed an Asian name. The introduction includes a lively defence of why he kept the poem after discovering this.)

Other aspects of current politics are rarely addressed directly with such fierceness. One exception is Raphael Rubinstein's long 'Poem Begun on a Train', on privacy and surveillance, which takes in Mandelstam's 'Stalin Epigram', *The Lady Vanishes* (a scribbled poem reaches "an intermediate state of being more concrete / than if I wrote it by fingertip on a steamy window"), Hugh MacDiarmid's wartime persecution, the unlikelihood of Amtrak having installed individual CCTV, and much else.

Overall I was left with an after-echo of form and fragmentation working together to reflect the multiplicity of real and virtual worlds. The same is broadly true of Salt's *Best*, though it contains fewer obviously formal poems (and less end-rhyme).

If *Best American* feels slightly less American than usual, *Best British* continues to show the American influence seen in its predecessors. Editor Emily Berry throws the net wide to include poems from various online magazines such as *Poems in Which*, *Prac Crit* and *tender*, so some middle-sized print ones are absent – but this reflects the quality of work being published online. She's netted few older, established British names (all women). Younger generations are well represented, including graduates of the Complete Works programme for black and ethnic minority poets. Much writing-related activity shows up in the biographies but not many academic posts.

The majority of poems in *Best British* make things new by strangeness – many have a feel of collage, of post-internet randomness or of hidden patterning and trains of thought. The tone tends to be edgier than in *Best American*. Some poems speak through highly confected personas, partly a legacy of what could be called School of Lumsden – younger writers taught and influenced by series editor Roddy Lumsden and his own reading of Americans including writers of the Gurlesque. A browse through the book releases varied voices saying, Look, look at this! Isn't it strange? and inviting us to gasp, to laugh... "A sort of continual movement between hysteria and bathos," says Berry in an interview with *The London Magazine*. Such voices at their strongest include Fran Lock's modern traveller-woman 'Melpomene': "I am a bad wife, a wanting quarry / of witless worry; lank rage, grim schlock, / and stroppy poverty"; also Amy Key, Melissa Lee-Houghton, Adam Lowe, Rebecca Perry, Heather Phillipson, Jack Underwood and Sophie Collins, whose 'Dear No. 24601' starts:

> The future is an eye that I don't dare look into
> Last night I dreamed I was a ball of fire
> and woke up on the wrong side of the room

Less eclectic, quietly intense poems make their own space, for example Karen McCarthy Woolf's lament for a stillborn son in 'Mort Dieu', Niall Campbell's 'Midnight' and Zaffar Kunial's 'The Word', which meditates on an immigrant father's not-strictly-correct English:

> That definite article, half right, half
> wrong, still present between *enjoy* and *life*.

Other poems stand out because they stretch poetry in new ways: the highly-strung, highly-patterned dialogue in Amy McCauley's 'Kadmea Touch Me' or Sophie Mayer's 'Silence, Singing', which uses, mostly, lyrical paragraphs (see Rankine's *Citizen*) about language and women's permitted behaviour, incorporating literary references from Iphigenia to Anne Carson:

> After all the words for kill, there is a silence. In the silence, singing.
> 'Vehment, cryeng' that men do not want to hear.

Mayer's collage-y estrangement is one way of writing political poetry amid so many non-poetry types of political discourse. As with *Best American*, only a few poems directly incorporate contemporary politics and climate change, as in Vahni Capildeo's 'Moss, for Maya' or through Kayo Chingonyi's museum-keeper in 'Legerdemain'; or use the language or concepts of contemporary science like Kathryn Maris's science-fiction speaker in 'It was discovered that gut bacteria were responsible'.

But maybe many poems in both *Best American* and *British* reveal a state of mind, an anxiety, while withholding the causes. So little in the world makes sense that a poet can sometimes only construct a meaningful poem from disparate elements and glancing references, working all the harder with imagery, lineation and other usual devices to draw the reader in.

I'm already regretting good poems this review has had to pass by... and I still remember one thing not bought in that street market – an umbrella whose wooden handle was carved with a Byzantine grapevine. It's much too soon to be sure which poems in these two *Best* anthologies will have staying power, and good to shelve the books alongside their predecessors to test this over the years. It is rumoured that Salt will discontinue *Best British Poetry* and 2015 may be the last. Let's hope not.

Fiona Moore's pamphlet Night Letter *is published by HappenStance.*

THE NATIONAL POETRY COMPETITION 2015

Judges: Sarah Howe, Esther Morgan, David Wheatley

T he judges share comments below on the top three winners in the National Poetry Competition 2015 – Eric Berlin, David Hawkins and Caroline Oxley. The poems are published for the first time in *TPR* and in the NPC anthology, which also contains the seven commended poems.

Sarah Howe on Eric Berlin's 'Night Errand'
When it first turned up in the pile, 'Night Errand' was one of those poems that wouldn't let you move on, but demanded a pause to dwell and recoup, followed by the compulsion to read it again. Its initial grip gave way to a sort of haunting. This is poetry that can somehow, magically, fill a cafeteria napkin dispenser with emotion, while subtly evoking the psychological need behind that displacement. Its syntax pays out like a wire, building to the final sting-in-the-tail: a realisation that deepens rather than diminishes what's gone before. In that complex moment, the poem refuses to let itself off the hook. Through its artful control of sound and line, its powers of image and perception, 'Night Errand' dramatises a cry of pain at the damage we're capable of doing to others.

David Wheatley on David Hawkins's 'Long Distance Relationship with a Mountain'
"*Dichten = condensare*" said Ezra Pound: writing poetry is all about condensation. It's certainly true of selecting poetry, as I discovered over the process of turning over 12,000 poems into 200 into 50 into 10. Michael Longley likes to refer to a part of the poet's anatomy he terms the "envy gland", and as I tried to select amid so many poems my envy gland proved invaluable. My hope is that other people too will read these poems and think: I wish I'd written that.

Do we write landscape poems or do they write themselves through us? 'Long Distance Relationship with a Mountain' is a poem of luminous mystery, not least in its human-natural interinanimations, in John Donne's word. This is poetry as field composition, assembling, mapping, "thinking with these hills" to summon the wonders of place into being before the reader's eyes.

Pound liked to divide poetry into three categories: *melopoeia* (the musical arrangement of sounds), *phanopoeia* (a casting of images on the visual imagination), and *logopoeia* (the dance of the intellect among words). Sadly Pound omitted to coin a term for poetry that combines all three, but taken as a whole this year's commended list does just that. The result is not just a song-cycle, but a symphony of sound and sense.

Esther Morgan on Carolyn Oxley's 'Biracial'
I'm glad we found space in our top three for the plain and poised speaking of Carolyn Oxley's 'Biracial'. It doesn't strain for effect, building its argument through a series of statements and the deployment of a beautifully judged simile ("The love that made you / was simple as the sounds / at breakfast"). The poem is far from simple, its dignified assertion of the right of an individual to be an individual complicated by that final risk-taking image. This balance between personal and public histories is what most impressed and moved us, articulated in a form and language that mirrors the daughter's straightness of spine.

. . .

National Poetry Competition 2015 Winners

First prize: Eric Berlin, 'Night Errand'
Second prize: David Hawkins,
 'Long Distance Relationship with a Mountain'
Third prize: Carolyn Oxley, 'Biracial'
Commended: Mara Adamitz Scrupe, 'Arillus'
Commended: Geraldine Clarkson, 'St Rose of Lima's Revenge'
Commended: Simon Jenner, 'Peter Philips' Part Book Talks to Brueghel'
Commended: Afra Kingdon, 'Tabasco'
Commended: Zaffar Kunial, 'Six'
Commended: Howard Laughton, 'Six Easy Calculations'
Commended: Fran Lock, 'Gentleman Caller'

ERIC BERLIN

Night Errand

O, Great Northern Mall, you dwindling oracle
of upstate New York, your colossal lot

of frost-heaved spaces so vacant I could cut
straight through while blinking and keep my eyes

shut, I've come like the flies that give up the ghost
at the papered fronts of your defunct stores,

through the food court where napkins, unused
to touch, are packed too tight to be dispensed,

past the pimpled kid manning the register
who stares at the buttons and wipes his palms.

If I press my eyes until checkers rise
from the dark – that's how the overheads glower

in home essentials as I roam through Sears,
seeking assistance. I know you're here.

For this window crank I brought, you show me
a muted wall of TVs where Jeff Goldblum

picks his way through the splintered remains
of a dinosaur crate. There must be fifty

of him, hunching over mud to inspect
the three-toed prints. I almost didn't

come in here at all, driving the opposite
of victory laps, and waiting as I hoped

for the red to leave my eyes, but my urgency
smacked of your nothingness. I did it again –

I screamed at the woman I love, and in front
of our one-year-old, who covered his ears.

DAVID HAWKINS

Long Distance Relationship with a Mountain

We got our hefting up here all right,
the wind curling round us visibly, curing us,
as if we were stones to be placed
and lichen-dappled with glacial deliberation.

And now, thinking with these hills,
a wandering sentence can be levelled
between them, tested against the mean
of wilful horizon and capricious sky.

Grey-brown green-black lutulent river
drawn easily as a snagged thread
pulling the best effects of the valley with it.
Light hurdles swiftly into huge stands of pines

and hides there with great abandon
intimate with the windage creaks and groans
in the crowns of these self-shredding trees
brashed and rusting beneath it.

Pulled back the thick curtain of moss
and found wheel ruts slanting
through the Ordovician, pulled back
at the false summit and wandered towards

a trig point decentred in the mist,
spectral sheep splayed tarsally among
the drop-skied moors, while someone else
is summiting surely in their own home-made uplands.

A snipe whittles up from a cloak of rushes
and I try to keep its ember alight with my eye
until with perfect clearance it falls
off the edge, or edges beyond seeing.

A particular breeze tugs its harmonic
adjusted to our hearing, we are earmarked,
as across the Irish sea a shadow range
of mountains echoes unsayably.

Here the so-called Black Road
on its endless ancient traverse over the ridge
intersects the local corpse road
that looks to another false summit

before the tireless sway of the Atlantic.
The real inheritance: looking at ravens,
waiting for their croak in the welcoming gloom.
The names of all the rocks make their own ground.

CAROLYN OXLEY

Biracial
for my daughter

Some people stare,
searching for a Judas bone,
but all they can find
are the stems of your arms,
the sleek plunge of femur
into socket.

These are the usual things,
and why shouldn't they be?
You were not a provision
of armistice or treaty.
You were not born to be
nation or diaspora.

The love that made you
was simple as the sounds
at breakfast: clink of pan
on stove, scraping-back of chair.
No slave ever rocked
inside the boat of your hips,
no explorer pried open
an African river.

They say the ancestors
reside in a sacred grove.
Your homeland is wherever
you stand. If the gaze lingers,
it's on your spine, straighter
than the fence lines
at Gettysburg.

Letter from the Isles of Scilly

BLUE VACANCY

Katrina Naomi

If you've ever been a writer-in-residence, or taken yourself off for a week's uninterrupted writing, you'll know something of that feeling of having everything just how you need it to write – being alone, no distractions, no phone or email, and a kettle nearby. You're incredibly enthusiastic and the words will come pouring out. I had a whole week as writer-in-residence on the Isles of Scilly, a place I'd never been to before.

Living in Penzance, I hear three sharp horn blows from *The Scillonian*, the Isles of Scilly ferry, as it sails every morning at 9.15, or thereabouts. I'd heard my friends talk about the Islands and I'd seen the bumps on the horizon on clear days on the bus to St Just. So when Goldsmiths College asked me to apply for research funding for a project, I got in touch with the Islands' school, and set myself up for a week's residency.

And of course you feel a fraud. I wanted to write but I wanted to explore St Mary's (the largest of the Islands), where *The Scillonian* docks and the tiny airplane lands. By "largest", we're not talking big. I walked around St Mary's coast path in six hours. But if it's not large, it's wild. It felt like a cross between West Penwith (the westernmost part of Cornwall where I live) and the view of the Summer Isles from north-western Scotland. I walked every day, built up a routine: reading first thing, then writing for the morning, a walk for most of the afternoon, then editing, then more reading (I read Tony Hoagland, Zaffar Kunial, Sara Maitland – and, don't laugh – *Robinson Crusoe*). I went to the pub on my first night, The Mermaid, in a gale, along the coast path by torch, alone. I felt safe walking in the dark, except for the wind, which could have blown me over but didn't.

As I said, you're meant to be working but want to explore. Always these push-and-pull factors on a residency. You tell yourself that you need to explore to respond to your surroundings, so the walks get longer. And the walking here is fantastic – if you ever go, walk to Halangy Down, a Neolithic, compact, terraced hamlet. And if you keep going to the north of the island, there's Innisdigen with its cairn and a wooded landscape you can really lose yourself in.

Apart from walking, and the occasional pub visit, the other distraction is the need to buy food. The Co op had little on the shelves that week – the shop was being refitted so half of it was closed, with no bread or fruit until the supply ship, *Gry Maritha*, arrived from Penzance. Almost everything is imported from the mainland, although you can buy veg, flowers and jam from roadside honesty stalls. I walked to the shop most days. I was staying out of the main town, Hugh Town, and wanted some interaction with people, no matter how limited. On my first day, I took a wrong turning, it was getting dark and I lost the path. I asked the way and a woman walked the ten or fifteen minutes to the shop with me – it's that sort of place.

I wanted to understand how the Islands worked, wanted to see if there were any boats going to St Agnes (among my friends in Penzance, most plump for St Agnes as being their favourite of the inhabited islands). And I'd met the landlady of St Agnes's Turk's Head on the horribly bumpy flight from Land's End airport (there being no ferry over a short period of the winter). She said to come over for tea. But there were no boats, other than the school boat bringing all the 'Off-Island' kids to St Mary's, and I didn't have the money to charter one. So I could only wonder about the other islands. And some days they were there and some days they weren't. The first day I saw St Martin's and the uninhabited Teän and Nornour, which were amazing. And then they disappeared again.

I hoped I might write about them. But I didn't. I hoped I might write in response to visiting Harold Wilson's grave. I didn't. I've started typing up what I wrote during that week; hard not to write about the sea on such a small island, but I found I often wrote about London and Penzance, among other things. It's too early to say if anything of these drafts will turn into half-decent poems. One or two have an air of something I can't quite catch at the moment, which may be promising. I need to wait.

And I did feel lonely. I always do on a residency. You turn in on yourself and I write at my best during these times, although I rarely feel it at the time. Once or twice during a month at Hawthornden Castle in Scotland last year, I felt excited about some early drafts – and sometimes I was right. These would go on to be poems I would publish and be proud of.

As part of the residency, I wanted to research poetry from the Islands. During an interview with Radio Scilly, I asked Island poets to get in touch. I had to walk up the hill every day after that to turn on my phone, pick up messages, phone people back and arrange to meet them. Most were humble about their own writing, "Oh you won't be interested in me, I'm not published or anything." Maureen Stuttaford and her twin told me about their writing group at the University of the Third Age over a bottle of wine in their roomy kitchen, battered by the wind. We talked about the idea of setting up a poetry trail on St Mary's. Jenny and John Purkess invited me to their home to talk about their late friend Tony Armstrong. There's a Radio 4 programme about his writing, which went out in 1981. I liked his work. 'The Wall on Old Town Hill' is a favourite – the wall's "complexion of lichen / Goes untalkative", with tobacco smoke disappearing "Into the blue vacancy of these mornings and afternoons". I also liked the stories the Purkesses told about their friend as they showed me a photo of a man in a roguish eyepatch. I met a builder, Todd Stevens, who wrote poems about shipwrecks, which he'd read to tourists on his boat 'ghost trips' to Rosevear Island, which is said to be haunted. The musician and songwriter Piers Lewin, from St Agnes, who I've yet to meet, has been an excellent correspondent, sending details on other poets for further research.

The most famous of the Islands' own poets is Robert Maybee, known as 'The Scillonian Poet', born and bred on St Mary's, who wrote during the nineteenth century, typically ballads about wrecks and the hardships of Scillonian life. David Constantine, who everyone referred to as "a proper poet", visits Bryher regularly; and Mary Wilson – Harold Wilson's widow – lives part of the year on St Mary's and is regarded with a good deal of affection. The Islands have a May festival of arts and literature, which I hope to return for and, if invited, give a talk on the poetry of the Islands (yes, coals to Newcastle and all of that).

Still, there's a reticence on the Islands to talk of one's own poetry. No sense of pushing yourself forwards as you might if you live in London or some other metropolis, very little interest in Twitter or Facebook or the dreaded LinkedIn (yes, all of which I post on). There's no Stanza group, not one member of The Poetry Society – I sensed locals all felt these were things for 'somewhere else'. The Islands are somewhere else. They are thirty miles off West Cornwall, which I'm frequently told is so far from everywhere (for which read London). I also sensed their pride in being different, of not quite being part of everywhere else. The day I was leaving a call went out on the radio for people to come and help fix the roof of one of the gig-rowing buildings at Porthmellon. Had I been staying on, I think I'd have volunteered. It's that sort of place. I might even have got a poem out of it.

Katrina Naomi is a post-doctoral researcher at Goldsmiths College, University of London. Her second collection, The Way the Crocodile Taught Me, *is published by Seren.*

CONTRIBUTORS

Howard Altmann has published two collections, *Who Collects the Days* (Mosaic Press, 2005) and *In This House* (Turtle Point Press, 2010). He lives in New York • **Rae Armantrout**'s new and selected poems, *Partly*, is due from Wesleyan UP in August • **Caroline Bird**'s latest collection is *The Hat-Stand Union* (Carcanet, 2013) • **A.K. Blakemore**'s first collection, *Humbert Summer*, was published by Eyewear in 2015 • **Miles Burrows** has won several awards in the Hippocrates Prize for Poetry and Medicine • **Chen Chen** was a finalist for a Ruth Lilly and Dorothy Sargent Rosenberg Poetry Fellowship in 2015 • **Patrick Cotter** won the Keats-Shelley Prize in 2013. He lives in Cork • **Claudia Emerson** (1957–2014) received the Pulitzer Prize for *Late Wife* in 2005 • **Suzannah Evans**'s pamphlet *Confusion Species* was a winner in the 2011 Poetry Business Competition • **Leontia Flynn**'s most recent collection is *Profit and Loss* (Cape, 2011) • **Dai George**'s first collection, *The Claims Office*, was published by Seren in 2013 • **David Hart**'s latest book, *Library Inspector or The One Book Library* (2015), is published by Nine Arches • **John Hennessy** is the author of *Coney Island Pilgrims* (Ashland Poetry Press, 2013) and *Bridge and Tunnel* (Turning Point Books, 2007) • **Ailish Hopper** is the author of *Dark-Sky Society* (New Issues, 2014) and the chapbook *Bird in the Head* (Center for Book Arts, 2005) • **A.B. Jackson** has published two collections, *Fire Stations* (Anvil, 2003) and *The Wilderness Party* (Bloodaxe, 2015) • **Nick Laird**'s third collection is *Go Giants* (Faber, 2013) • **Patrick Mackie**'s *The Further Adventures of the Lives of the Saints* is forthcoming from CB Editions • **Cate Marvin**'s books include *World's Tallest Disaster* (Sarabande Books, 2001) and *Oracle* (W.W. Norton, 2015) • **Thomas McCarthy**'s next collection, *Pandemonium*, will be published by Carcanet in 2017 • **Richard O. Moore** (1920–2015) was a filmmaker and poet. A selection of his poems, *Writing the Silences* (2010), is published by University of California Press • **Tomás Q. Morín**'s *A Larger Country* (Copper Canyon) received the APR/Honickman Prize in 2012 • **Rebecca Perry**'s first collection, *Beauty/Beauty* (Bloodaxe, 2015), was shortlisted for the T.S. Eliot Prize • **Pascale Petit**'s next collection, *Mama Amazonica*, will be published by Bloodaxe in 2017 • **Rachel Piercey** has published two pamphlets with The Emma Press, *The Flower and the Plough* and *Rivers Wanted* • **Donald Revell**'s latest collection is *Tantivy* (Alice James Books, 2012) • **Atsuro Riley**'s *Romey's Order* (University of Chicago Press, 2010) received the Kate Tufts Discovery Award • **Christopher Robley** is an award-winning poet and indie-pop songwriter. He lives in Maine • **Karen Solie**'s *The Road In Is Not the Same Road Out* (2015) is published by Anansi and by FSG. *The Living Option: Selected Poems* is published by Bloodaxe • **Danez Smith**'s *[insert] boy* (YesYes Books, 2014) received the Lambda Literary Award and the Kate Tufts Discovery Award. *Don't Call Us Dead* is due from Graywolf in 2017 • **Matthew Sweeney**'s latest collection is *Inquisition Lane* (Bloodaxe, 2015) • **Jamila Woods** is a member of the Dark Noise collective. She received a Ruth Lilly and Dorothy Sargent Rosenberg Poetry Fellowship in 2015.

Periplum

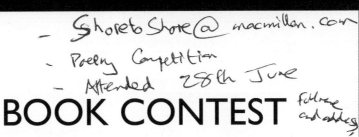

Handwritten notes:
- ShoretoShore@macmillan.com
- Poetry Competition
- Attended 28th June
- Followee and address

BOOK CONTEST

£1000 to the winner +
publication in our new series

Open to all poets

See our website for full guidelines and to submit
www.plymouth.ac.uk/periplum

Series Editor / Judge: Anthony Caleshu

Deadline 1st September 2016

Periplum Poetry Pamphlets for 2016:
Mark Ford, Peter Gizzi, and Eiléan Ní Chuilleanáin

**POETRY
WITH
PLYMOUTH
UNIVERSITY**

THE 2016 UNIVERSITY OF CANBERRA
VICE-CHANCELLOR'S INTERNATIONAL POETRY PRIZE

FIRST PRIZE $15,000
ENTER BY 30 JUNE 2016

The head judge for 2016 will be Simon Armitage.
For more details please visit the prize website:
canberra.edu.au/vcpoetryprize

Recognising creative excellence

UNIVERSITY OF
CANBERRA

The Poetry Review
Spring launch at Keats
House, London

Join us in the beautiful surroundings
of Keats House to hear readings
by **Emily Berry**, **Caroline Bird**,
A.K. Blakemore and **David Hart**

Thursday 28 April 2016
6.30pm-8.30pm. Readings from 7pm

Keats House, 10 Keats Grove
London NW3 2RR

Nearest station: Hampstead Heath

Tickets are free but must
be reserved in advance at
tinyurl.com/jpfrgsb

THEPOETRYSOCIETY

MA in Writing Poetry

A ground-breaking collaboration between Newcastle University and the Poetry School: a Master's degree in Writing Poetry

- Two years part time
- Starting September 2016
- Firmly rooted in the publishing, performing and promoting poetry world
- Competitively priced: £2,750 per year
- Unique combination of small group and individual teaching
- Study in Newcastle or London
- Newcastle tutors include Sean O'Brien, Jacob Polley and W N Herbert
- Newcastle teaching centre - full student amenities, access to Newcastle Centre of Literary Arts' event programme
- London tutors include Roddy Lumsden, Clare Pollard and Tamar Yoseloff
- London teaching centre - close to Saison Poetry Library and other central London cultural hubs, at the heart of a thriving poetry community
- Newcastle and London students come together for an annual joint Summer School
- MA features guest tutors from the Poetry School's established teaching community

All teaching arrangements are subject to confirmation

Applications are now open, for further information please email John Canfield at **coordinator@poetryschool.com** (for study in London) or Melanie Birch at **Melanie.Birch@newcastle.ac.uk** (for study in Newcastle) or visit the application portal at **www.ncl.ac.uk**